A book of happy accidents and improvisations that would be a lovely addition to any teacher's bookshelf ...

Ian McMillan, poet, broadcaster and comedian

Learning is natural; sometimes it gets difficult and then the learner gets stuck. When we get stuck we need a teacher who makes it feel natural to want to get learning again. Hywel Roberts is one of these. In real life he is a teacher who finds the way to open doors, include the loner, create the hook or dilemma that cannot be side-stepped ... the sort of teacher who entices the learner and reduces resistance.

His book talks with the reader, the teacher who wants to think again about how they are in the classroom, around the school and in the staffroom. The stream of ideas for engaging with pupils and making learning live are supported by a down-to-earth conversation about how it really is in the day-to-day life of the school. It makes you smile, wince, laugh, and ponder ... and most of all think: think how enjoyable teaching can be if we invest in ourselves as teachers.

Open it anywhere ... it is full of gems.

Mick Waters, Professor of Education at Wolverhampton University

It's no accident that Hywel Roberts – himself a world leader in enthusiasm – has written a must read book for teachers. *Oops! Helping children learn accidentally* brings together insight, pizzazz, wit and quirkiness into one happy place, it's a joy of a book written by a great teacher. Easy to read, practical, full of great ideas and invention – it's more than a book, it's a treatise on positivity and a reminder of why it's great to be a teacher.

Alistair Smith, learning consultant and author, www.alistairsmithlearning.com

There can be little doubt that the new book Hywel has written is tantalising, and so useful for the new teacher. It will, I am sure, stand alongside iconic publications that hit the 'common touch' as the truth is so sharp in the contexts he writes and explores.

Hywel has, at long last, launched a war on the 'drains', i.e. those mis-named teachers who glory in pouring toxic substances all over anything 'child centred' in schooling, and shrieks like a Greek Siren the awful warning that to ignore the drawing power of these malice makers means professional death.

I liked the text a lot as it reminded me of all the wonderful moments in my teaching career – the fun, the joy of working with spotty youth, the challenges of facing the classes almost impossible to teach and finding a way to get through.

We hear the voice of a true pioneer, clear and sure in the belief that teaching is an amalgam of so many things beyond 'subject knowledge'. The book races along at an almost breathless speed – just like the writer.

I am envious that this book has been written so well and captures so much.

In all the showers of experience that Hywel brings the reader, we see a humility born out of experience and a deep knowing of young people. We also know that the book has been written from first-hand experience – so rare in today's awful target-driven texts. Hywel has much experience in an area of woeful economic deprivation after the closure of the steel industry, as well as the deepening depression occurring in the north.

But no 'doom and gloom' indulgences are allowed. We are reminded of the continuing professional responsibility of bringing learning to life and we keep getting very clear guidance for newcomers as well as reminders for us oldies of how we have to keep vigilant to make our teaching count.

Luke Abbott, Director of Mantle of the Expert

As someone who struggles to finish educational literature, I knew I was onto a winner early on when Morrissey and *Jaws'* Chief Brody were key references.

This book had Hywel Roberts' inspirational stamp of wit and infectious enthusiasm running right through its core; I read the whole book with a huge grin on my face, often laughing out loud or whispering, 'Aw, I love that!' I felt like I had been let in on his secret and I had - it's a mindset, not a technique. Where else would you be instructed to ensure that 'Happiness' was in your curriculum?

Hywel's emphasis on connecting at a human level ensures children have a relevant and memorable experience with a real person, whom he encourages to be brave and embrace the unexpected and in turn empower pupils to question and steer their own learning. It's so steeped in common sense that you can't disagree with it!

The novel illustrations, acronyms and lists really made me chuckle; I promise to now 'embrace the emo kid'. The subtle reinterpretations of popular sayings kept me on my toes, although my mind didn't wander once. What would take many people half a page to say, Hywel encapsulates in one word or drawing. I have come away with a whole new vocabulary to tap me on the shoulder as I plan and teach, to remind me of my purpose and keep me on track.

Rather than lesson plans and schemes of work, there are inspiring anecdotes from all phases, so there are no 'get outs'; he has succeeded at luring children of all ages and backgrounds into actively learning.

As I read, not only did I constantly reflect on my own 'botheredness' but kept adding to the internal list I was forming of people to buy this for. At a time in my career when I am filled with self-doubt and fear, this book is like a magic medicine that reminds me why I became a teacher and empowers me to buy a stack of sticky notes and fat pens and start 'digging', 'luring' and 'raving' in my own classroom on Monday morning.

In short, it's BLUMMIN' BRILLIANT!

Ruth Saxton, Primary School Teacher and Chair for NATD

Quirky, creative and personable, Hywel is a gifted teacher with a passion for enabling others. In this gem of a book he shares his passion for captivating children through memorable learning experiences. If you want the children in your school to make great progress and remember you as a teacher who made learning fun, dip into this book for inspiration and ideas.

Diane Heritage, Deputy Lead Associate, North of England National College

Reading Hywel's book has been a pleasure. As a primary teacher for over twenty years, with the additional role of 'Creativity Coordinator' tagged on for good measure, I was 'hooked' by the first sentence of the foreword: 'Good teachers are great liars'! I immediately wanted to know more, and especially as I've been lucky enough to hear Hywel present training to teachers, the 'preferably read it with a Barnsley accent' had me intrigued.

The last thing I need is book about teaching theory; no busy teacher needs that. We get enough theory and hoops to jump through from senior management, Government initiatives and the continual pressure of the inspectors arriving to give ourselves more reading for reading's sake. Hywel's book is not like that. Yes, it contains theory, it talks about learning and child-centredness but it is also inspiring, easy to read and is filled to the rafters with practical application; things I can steal and adapt for my learners and for me; things that actually work and will invigorate my teaching practice without it once making me doubt my own ability. Things that have made me go 'hmmmm?!'.

As I read through the book (literally from cover to cover) I was struck by the cleverness of the 'Lists'. Hywel writes lists and bullet points throughout. 'Top 10s' and 'Top 5s', Lists of the Bests and the Worsts, Things-to-do, Things-not-to-do, bullet-pointed action points and superb summing-ups. All of these appeal to me, and are RELEVANT. Relevance is a recurring theme. The book contains simple, effective illustrations, brilliant 'sliding scales' to provoke thought and reflection on who and where I am as a teacher and I acknowledge to myself now that I will be recommending Hywel's book to so many of my colleagues: from students and NQTs who will absorb and adapt the suggestions without resistance, to the older switched-off colleagues who have arrived at the point of forgetting what the point is in being the teacher and lead learner. The book offers something for everyone engaged in education, whether that engagement is currently active or not. It is for those of us who love teaching and are instinctively creative in what we do but always want to be better at it. It is also, most importantly, for those who are not sure how to be creative, or how to liven the classroom and the learning for which we are responsible. And for those who may have accidentally switched to standby, waiting for something or someone to reactivate them, this is that switch.

I would regard myself as BRAVE (read the book to find out what Hywel means by this) but I will go back to this for inspiration and to refresh my teaching over and over. I would like to thank Hywel on behalf of my future pupils, who will undoubtedly pass through my classes and accidently learn more than they would have if I had not read this book.

Susan Coates, St Gregory's RC Primary School, South Shields

Oops! must be essential reading for student teachers. It is a dossier for practical teaching and describes the pedagogy of 'the buzzing'. Hywel Roberts offers a book that is a filled to capacity with drama-led ideas that are far from a performance and without a leotard in sight. I am buying a copy for each of the team at school.

Richard Kieran, Headteacher, Woodrow First School

What fun!! This book is packed full of practical ideas to make your classroom an engaging, exciting and fun place to be – whatever the age of your pupils. Less is more when it comes to teaching and learning: less teacher direction and control – more learning for the learners.

Hywel makes the art of questioning, waiting and trusting learners to rise to the situation safer and less scary for teachers. Go on – try one or two of his ideas ... they really work.

I'm so tempted to go back to the classroom to use more of Hywel's brilliant and inspiring ideas with young learners. I'll certainly be using his techniques with the groups of leaders I work with. I know they will make me better at helping people learn.

Enjoy. I intend to ...

Thank you Hywel.

Karen Ardley, Karen Ardley Associates

This is a book of 'substance' (not that sort!) which speaks to you with formidable experience and gregarious humour. Examples of Hywel's experience are interwoven throughout the chapters. As is the humour! Hywel highlights the essence of enjoyment, necessary for all learners, including the teachers. Inspirational ideas spill as the book progresses and all written in such a direct style that you cannot help but 'see the light'. Great thanks indeed go to Hywel for being so generous in sharing his experiences. A must-read for all who work with children.

Julie Bruck, Advanced Skills Teacher, Barnsley

It's fair to say that we sometimes get books that we think we **ought** to read, trust me this is a book that you will **want** to read! I read it in two sittings as I couldn't put it down – cliché? – well I defy you to start reading it and see for yourself. It should come with a few warnings though:

Don't read it in a public place – you will get strange looks when you sit there laughing out loud!

This book will cause you to question your own teaching, methods, approaches and motivation – be prepared to do some serious thinking about your own classroom. When was the last time you 'lured' your pupils into their learning? Hywel talks about 'igniting curiosity', 'capturing imagination' and 'botheredness'!

As a result of your thinking – this book will then cause you more soul-searching as you begin to take risks – stepping out of your comfort zone is never easy!

One of the key strengths of this book is that it's written by a practising teacher – one who 'gets it', who is dealing with a whole range of pupils and their attitudes – it's not a 'worthy tome by someone who hasn't been in a classroom for years' … it's amazing the number of times he hits the nail on the head. The positivity of this book is really refreshing; patience, being a radiator not a drain, what is MY usp … some of these I know but I just needed reminding as it's easy to get tired and lack the energy to be creative and BRAVE!

However, to borrow one of Hywel's favourite words – you'll be 'buzzing' when you've read this!

Buzzing with ideas, enthusiasm, a sense of 'I want to give that a go' … definitely a read for teachers who want to be reinspired! I want to be that 'positive teacher', excuse me while I just reread …… Oops!

PS please read page 25 – number 1 – that's me … I'm officially a good teacher ☺ as I just LOVE stationery shops!

Jane Hewitt, AST Dearne ALC, Barnsley and affiliate of *Creative Teaching & Learning* magazine

At last there is a book to cover all bases. Whether you are a student teacher, NQT or school leader, this is a genuine guide to push your own practice. Do you want to be an outstanding teacher? Do you want to lead an outstanding school? Read this book and your life will be a whole load easier. I'd like to think that all the 'Drains' who sit in staffrooms throughout the country will soon be reading this book in their PPA time instead of perusing the tabloid press or playing chess!

Hywel Roberts combines his knowledge of cutting-edge pedagogy with humour and genuine experience to provide an unpretentious guide to teaching. Reading this book made me laugh, remember the dark days of my own education and some memories of my early days in the classroom. It also made me nod, think, reflect, learn and enthuse about the job we all do. If you are a teacher, or want to be a teacher, please read this book!

Dave Whitaker, Executive Deputy Headteacher, Springwell Community School

Oops! is about principles. It's about a mentality that encourages us to drop the reins of rigid, boring schemes of work and instead create learning that is exciting and relevant! Via practical ideas, anecdote and dry wit, Roberts' magnificent work dares us to believe that we can make it so.

Jamie Portman, Assistant Headteacher, Campsmount Technology College

Educators! Look to your laurels! There's a hip, young(ish) gunslinger coming at ya straight outta Barnsley, and he's gonna change the way you think! Hywel Roberts is a magpie's intellect writing like a man with two brains on a heavyweight jag of a particularly garrulous amphetamine. His message is that engagement is the message and in delivering it he's sharp, he's intellectually underpinned, he's effervescent, he's the teacher you wished your teachers had seen teach.

In *Oops! Helping Children Learn Accidentally* he's produced a cornucopic (I know it doesn't exist – it should) antidote to cynicism; a call to arms. It's part memoir, part guide, part surreal series of disembodied lists, part methodology for being the kind of maverick who gets better results than anyone else and that the kids like better than they like you (!) Read it, shed your teaching skin, and there'll be no danger that you'll ever, ever become what Hywel memorably calls, 'A monkey. A puppet. A monkey puppet.'

Phil Beadle, Teacher, Education Consultant and Author

Oops!

Hywel Roberts

Oops!

Helping children learn accidentally

Edited by Ian Gilbert

Independent Thinking Press

Published by
Independent Thinking Press, Crown Buildings, Bancyfelin, Carmarthen, Wales,
SA33 5ND, UK
www.independentthinkingpress.com

Independent Thinking Press is an imprint of Crown House Publishing Ltd.

© Hywel Roberts, 2012
Cover photograph © Jane Hewitt, 2012
(www.janehewittphotography.co.uk)
Illustrations © istockphoto, 4khz

British Library of Cataloguing-in-Publication Data
A catalogue entry for this book is available from the British Library.

Print ISBN 978-1-78135-009-6
Mobi ISBN 978-1-78135-039-3
ePub ISBN 978-1-78135-040-9

Edited by Ian Gilbert
Designed and typeset by Heidi Baker
Printed and bound in the UK by Gomer Press, Llandysul, Ceredigion

For Maria and Tom: everything to me

Foreword

Good teachers are great liars. They create all sorts of untruths, weaving a whole tangled web of deception on a daily basis in order to trick children into learning, despite their best intentions to the contrary. They lie. They cheat. They deceive. They hoodwink. And they have their own language of deceit too. 'Let's imagine ...'. 'Let's pretend ...'. 'What if ... ?'.

In order to go through the artificial process of teaching children about things that aren't there (volcanoes, poverty, desert islands, molecules, God ...) they have to act as if they were there.

Lies, all lies.

To make the lies work, that is to say to ensure they remain invisible, the duplicitous teacher must also ensure the learners join in the deceit too. 'If you were a poor abandoned dog, how would you be feeling at this moment?' is a question whose structure guarantees that children have to join in the lie in order to respond. 'But I'm not a dog!' won't help. 'But if I were a dog, I'm sure I would be too cute to be abandoned' is better. Just.

This is what good teachers do. They create alternative possibilities, different realities, ones that are enticing to young minds, ones that lure children in. Teacher as Child Catcher.

(Poor quality teachers, on the other hand, think their job is to impart knowledge, dry facts that are as real as that volcano they are studying on the other side of the world and remain just as distant.)

Children may learn real facts about real volcanoes but they will absorb and remember everything there is to know about made-up volcanoes that could erupt at any time in the corner of the classroom. In the science of memory, context memory (real-life learning) trumps content learning ('"Fact, fact, fact!" repeated Thomas Gradgrind.') every time. Deceit is what is used to make it real. Want them to know about the truth? Start with lies. Works every time.

Hywel Roberts' pants are usually on fire. He is a master fabulist, a weaver of complete and utter nonsense (flying machines, talking dogs, mad women on supposedly uninhabited islands ...). His ability to make lies out of facts knows no bounds. Whenever he sees something real he likes the look of – a photo, a story, an object, a toy – the question first to his treacherous mind is this one:

Where's the curriculum in that?

In other words, how can I exploit this discovery and turn it into a fantasy to trick children into learning? This is what *Oops!* is all about – the ability to pluck the curriculum from the environment, wrap it up in a tissue of lies for the classroom and trick children into learning about it. Oops!, I just taught you something while we were having fun and making stuff up. Oops!, I just learned something and I came to school today determined to repel all assaults on my ignorance. Damn you, Mr Roberts!!

Drama is a great way of lying to children but, although Hywel draws from his experience of using drama to help children learn well, this is not a book about drama in the classroom. Far from it. This book – best read in a Barnsley accent wherever possible – is full of ideas and activities to bring the learning alive in many, many ways and will seriously challenge the nature of your teaching.

So, read this book, seek out the curriculum that is found all around you, take it, then turn it into a big fat lie with which to trick your children into learning everything there is about it.

And may God have mercy on your soul.

Ian Gilbert
Santiago
March 2012

Acknowledgements

Thanks to ... Jane Hewitt for taking my picture and for being the teacher we all wish we could be. David Whitaker for being the good guy on the side of vulnerable kids. Luke Abbott for opening so many doors and for being Dorothy Heathcote's outstanding Sherpa. Karen Ardley for helping me to hold my nerve. Mick Waters, Jamie Portman, Alistair Smith, John Turner and others who have given me wonderful opportunities through gainful employment. The National Association for the Teaching of Drama (NATD) for inspiration and for fighting hard for teachers and the teaching of Drama. Matthew Milburn for the permission to be the teacher I could be (and to stop simply making up plays) as well as for the Chilean miners' lesson. Tim Godwin for his 'Northern bloke' impressions. Helen Toft for her passion and for helping people to be brilliant. Liz Gaughan and Dave Matthews at Horbury School back in the day. Melanie Cutler for hoovering the taxi rank. Iona Towler-Evans, Ondrie Mann, Gemma Handley, Tim Taylor and Richard Kiernan – the Mantle experts. Phil Beadle for telling me I should write a book. Diane and Russell Heritage for helping me let go. Darren and Ronnie at Enquire. Debbie Kidd for unlocking potential in children and teachers. Verity Watts for pushing my thinking. Josie Thirkell, Simon Barber, Phil Davies and Marc Doyle for giving me work at the start. Staff and students at Springwell Community Special School and the Kingstone School, Barnsley, UK.

Also a heartfelt thanks to those friends and family who've demonstrated interest mixed with a dash of patience during the writing of this book. Nainy and Jackie Butterfly. Cheers also to my soundtrack of King Creosote, Ron Sexsmith, the Manic Street Preachers and James. Hi to Jason Isaacs!

Big thanks to my editor, the kind Ian Gilbert, who believed I had something to say, and for tirelessly, honestly and supportively helping me to fulfil my ambition of writing a book. And Caroline Lenton and her team at Independent Thinking Press for their advice, support and enthusiasm.

And especially to my Dad, Arfon Roberts, who would have loved this silliness.

Contents

- Don't smile until Christmas

Stop Teaching Me When I'm Trying to Learn

When dealing with people, remember you are dealing with creatures of emotion, not creatures of logic.

Dale Carnegie

Get a room full of teachers together. Ask them to talk to each other about *teaching*. Watch their faces fall as they speak. Observe the heads that shake and the shoulders that shrug. Watch them indicate with their hands the current frustrations they feel – kids, government, leadership, time, resources. Listen as the silence falls when they look to you to move the meeting on.

Right … Get a room full of teachers together. Ask them to share with each other their *guilty pleasures* (nothing too dark!).

 Teacher guilty pleasures (that I've heard from teachers themselves)

1   *Carry On* films (in particular *Camping*, *Cleo* and *Screaming*)

2   All things David Essex

3   Reality TV

4   Bon Jovi

5   A chocolate fountain in the living room

6   Bubble bath

7   Dolly Parton

8   Black-and-white horror films

9   Line dancing

10 Musicals (not the namby-pamby modern stuff though)

Now notice how they behave differently to before. Look at how they chortle and talk. Watch how they animate themselves. Observe how they share funny stuff. Stop them and ask them to move to another conversation partner. Invite them to share their guilty pleasures whilst sharing what they've heard from their other colleagues. Let the gossip run and encourage them to wallow in the fun. Listen to the laughter. Notice the engagement. They're lured in: hook, line and thinker. You'll have to call them to order. Move on ...

Okay ...

So, what's this book about? Well, one of the toughest groups you will ever have to engage in learning are your colleagues. As Kevin Rowland of Dexys Midnight Runners said, 'Let's get this straight from the start'. If you can get *them* hooked into learning then the world is your lobster. Sadly, this book is not about engaging your colleagues. Thankfully, it's about engaging the children in your classroom. And they're the toughest group there is.

When I became a teacher I was given the schemes of work and left to get on with it, which I dutifully did. In a way it was a great way to get a career going in that you learned on the job. A bit like fishmongery. Or debt-collecting. Except with twelve weeks off a year. I taught English and Drama. They are the subjects I've stayed loyal to and in which I have seen numerous developments over the last couple of decades. I've also taught Media Studies, Dance (I know) and, due to a timetabling error, Music. More recently, I taught as part of a team delivering a 'blended curriculum' for 11- to 13-year-olds – more of that later. The reason I'm telling you this is because *I am a teacher* – I'm not just some bloke in a suit who has done lots and lots of research. I'm not full-time in one school now, but I am part-time in many.

Looking back to the time when I first stepped into a classroom, a key development has been the movement of focus in education from *teaching* to *learning and teaching*. This is what this book is about: engaging teaching that lets the children learn, often in unpredictable ways that no one envisaged, especially them. Hence the term 'accidental learning'.

What this book isn't about

1   Chucking out your current curriculum

2   Punching the air and shouting, 'Come on! Let's do it for the kids!'

3   Egg sucking

4 Ignoring the demands of subject coverage and external accountability

5 Upsetting your head teacher (if you are a member of staff)

6 Upsetting your staff (if you are a head teacher)

7 Making stuff up as you go along

8 Preparing for inspection

9 Using textbooks effectively

10 Playing the bagpipes

What this book *is* about

1 Raising your game in the classroom around learning and teaching

2 Being *brave*

3 Enabling independent thinking

4 Getting children to *expect* to learn when they're with you

5 Getting a bigger boat

6 Finding conventional curriculum in unconventional places

7 Tricking children into deep learning

8 Embracing the unpredictable

9 The choreography behind an engaging curriculum, tried and tested

10 Catchy lists

Here's a list of people I've worked with over the last few months who have helped me to hone the ideas in this book (so don't tell me they don't or can't work):

- Sixteen-year-olds on their first day as sixth-formers in a brand new building

- A team of teachers for a session on using the curriculum to manage behaviour. Among the assembled were teachers who teach all ages – from 4 to 16+, home tutors and a bloke who teaches sex offenders life skills. Now that was differentiation and personalised learning wrapped up in a five-hour session

- Teachers working in a school for children with social and emotional difficulties

- Children who are in 'danger' of failing their final examinations

- Drama skills for non-Drama teachers

- A load of timetablers at a timetabler conference (honestly, it was buzzing)

- A conference for PE teachers

- Five-year-olds rescuing a really scary cat from a tree

- A team of artists interested in working more closely with schools

- A secondary school staff. Nothing out of the ordinary there perhaps, except it was a twilight session. And the inspectors were watching

The constant theme throughout this list is *learning*. As professionals we need to keep learning in the same way a shark needs to keep moving, otherwise it'll die. When we stop learning, cynicism can seep in and pretty soon we start hating kids. This book will help to keep us moving forward and my hope is that it will offer you the opportunity to reflect on your own practice.

None of what I offer here requires you to chuck out schemes of work that you feel are tried and tested. It does however suggest that you could look at said schemes from a different perspective. Nor am I attacking the need for lesson objectives, thorough planning or measureable outcomes; what I am offering is a different way to offer *content* to support appropriate *coverage*.

I have drawn my inspiration for this approach from a variety of sources, including the late Dorothy Heathcote's Mantle of the Expert system. This is a fantastic approach to teaching and learning which places the child at the centre of an *enterprise* by being a member of a *responsible team*. It's been a massive influence on me and I encourage you to look at the website www.mantleoftheexpert.com, run by Luke Abbott and Tim Taylor, for more information. The head teacher of my last school invited Dr Heathcote into our school years ago and she had a profound impact on my view of learning, teaching and engagement. She stopped me simply making up plays and enabled me to use Drama properly.

Now, before you stick this book back on the shelf because I've mentioned the D-word, think again; the briefest enquiry into the work of Heathcote, Abbott and others will reveal that the Mantle of the Expert actually encompasses the *entire curriculum*. It's a genuine tool for teachers, and there are many resources available on the website I've mentioned. This isn't a book about the Mantle of the Expert; rather, it takes some of its inspiration from it. If the ideas in this book float your boat, then I urge you to seek out the system.

The reason I've written this book is to share some ideas with you. As teachers we are constantly in search of resources and it's great when something we discover genuinely works in a real classroom with real children and young people. All of the ideas here are genuine and are designed for you to take away, adapt and make work in your own classroom, whether you teach the youngest or the oldest. The reason I'm confident with this view is because this book not only offers ideas, but also offers ways of thinking, planning and delivering. It offers an approach that is rooted in solid expectations, productive classroom management and inductive teaching.

Remember that moment at a theme park when you're strapped into the roller coaster and then launched off at high speed? You're stuck there and for the next three minutes or so you are at the mercy of a predetermined journey. As soon as it's over, you are released and free to go. This, to me, is what many a child's experience of school is like – with the exception that roller coasters can at least be memorable and, for a few quid, you get a picture of yourself screaming. We need to look at the learning journeys we are offering our children and ensure that they don't emulate the roller coaster experience. We can create learning that places the child at the centre of the action where much of what happens can emerge through a supportive classroom climate, clever questioning and irresistible lures. Much of what is on offer here is based around happy *learning accidents*. Objectives and outcomes can be clear but we also need to embrace the unexpected and allow a deeper curriculum to emerge between them. In this book I'll show you how.

 **Accidental discoveries**

1   LSD

2   Ice lollies

3   The microwave oven

4   Post-it notes

5   Penicillin

6   Teflon

7   Brandy

8   Potato crisps

9   Artificial sweetener

10 Viagra

- Always be nice to the Emo kid

The
Human
App

Charity Boxing Night Ends in Brawl

Keighley News

People are great, aren't they? You can probably play out the story behind the headline in your own imagination: can you see the charity fight going on, the bell signalling the end of a round, the people shaking collection buckets for change? Then can you sense the tension? Something clicks and suddenly everything kicks off. The referee jumps out of the ring whilst members of the audience leap in, fists flying, and the two boxers look on bemused. Sense and sensibility are sidelined in favour of aggression and anger.

I, Robot

I recently worked with a class of 10- and 11-year-olds during which I told them I had received a message from the government saying that teachers were going to be replaced by androids. I described the androids as Terminator-esque and really cool. You will be able to see through that but remember these were 10-year-olds. Straight away, the children were hooked in – in particular the hard-to-reach-but-biddable boys. I had thrown a *context* at them using the lure of a government message. This bait grips the children so that learning can take place within that context. The context is the fiction that surrounds the lure itself which the teacher can develop in line with their own aims and objectives. If we were to broaden this out to a process, this is what it might look like:

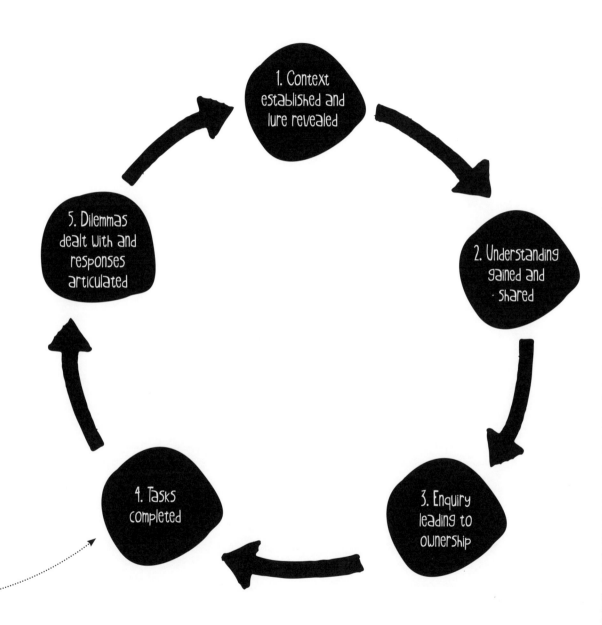

Let me explain further. This *lure process* invites children to share their own view of the world and their place within it by promoting enquiry, questioning, problem-solving, empathy and empowerment. In creating a lure process the teacher needs to begin with the curriculum: What learning is required by the class? What skills do my children need to achieve my objectives? What do I want the learning to look like in my classroom? What strategies and techniques can I use to metaphorically leave the classroom?

In establishing a lure, it is important to choose something that will grip a class – something that will ignite curiosity and inquisition. Through skilled application, the lure can become a vessel of deep learning and open up various opportunities for children to articulate responses. These could be written, spoken, drawn or sung – the key to the response is that it will be *human* and *authentic*.

Back to teacher terminators ...

The regular class teacher I was supporting wanted the children to look at how they learn in class, what was important to them and what they wanted the relationship with the teacher to be like in order to get the most out of their time in class (CLASS = Come in Late And Start Sleeping).

Using the model, this is what happened.

1   **Context established and lure revealed:** In my role as a secretive government official, I bring a letter to the class and share it. This is the lure. It reveals that the government has plans to replace all teachers with androids and the views of the children are being canvassed. After the initial excitement, the questions begin. The official, known as Mr X, then asks the children to 'sign' an Official Secrets Act. They do this by placing their thumb print on a piece of paper passed around the room. One question asked is 'Can I tell my Mum and Dad?' Mr X replies, 'They already know.'

2   **Understanding gained and shared:** Mr X is challenged by the teacher as to why this particular class has been chosen and he responds that it is because they are brilliant. The class are then invited to construct a list of questions that they wish to ask Mr X before he has to leave. They are directed away from low level questions and are challenged to get to the root of why human teachers are being disposed of.

3   **Enquiry leading to ownership:** By playtime the class have been successfully lured into the fiction and have feelings of being special – chosen. They are taking it seriously and feel that whatever is going on belongs to them. The interview exercise has deepened the fiction and has enabled a task to be set:

What traits do the androids need to enable you to be great learners?

The question itself is operating on a relatively high level and it is one that the teacher supports the learners through in terms of understanding. The task requires the children to work in groups towards a presentation in response to the question, as well as the overall context within which they are learning.

4   **Tasks completed:** Following Mr X's departure (where the 'fiction' was revealed as just that), the teacher helps with the construction of the presentations, but not the content. Essentially the children are offering their perspectives on good teaching and learning through the lens of the story. The teacher is seeing this during the development of the presentations.

5   **Dilemmas dealt with and responses articulated:** On leaving, Mr X says he will return in a few days with Professor Y, the inventor of the androids. This will be the day the presentations are showcased. Through the week the children are challenged by the deadline, but the key point is that they also start making their minds up about things:

They don't want androids as teachers.

They realise they need to voice this to Mr X. When Messrs X and Y arrive, the presentations take place. All children speak, participate and share. Perhaps even more important than the presentations are the discussions facilitated by the adults that take place afterwards.

You'll notice another adult was brought into the context. There are plenty of adults floating around your school so get them in if you can and give them something to do. Here's what the learning looked like:

• High order questioning

• 'Passenger' children speaking up and voicing thoughts

- Group work
- Shared responsibilities and roles
- Creative
- Inclusive
- Thinking time
- Dealing with dilemmas

In all, the response to the key question was essentially: we don't want android teachers, but *this* is what we want our teachers to be like. We want *real people* who are knowledgeable, caring, happy, firm and *unprogrammed*! During discussions with the class, this spectrum was created *by them*:

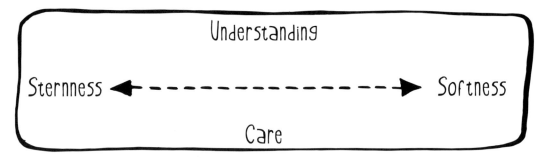

The class want their teachers to always treat them with care and understanding and to do this consistently. There is a shared understanding that teachers will veer or shift on the sliding scale between being stern (*firm*) and soft (*gentle*). This is what the children wanted from their teachers: a *human application*.

This is the result of a fictional context influencing the real world – the world of the child. So the next time you're planning a starter, as you may need to do four or five times a day, seek out something simple that will distract the children and trap them in your intended learning. Choose something that provokes questions, captures imagination and demonstrates a link to a real world outside the classroom. The young people will thank you for it. Given enough time, even the educational experts could perhaps come up with this. It would probably cost more money however.

Could you construct a piece of work that captures what children *want* out of your lessons? Could you lure them into doing this?

Think about:

- Capturing imagination
- Links to the world outside the classroom
- A compelling context
- Involving other colleagues
- Presenting the results
- How would this fulfil your school's Pupil Voice agenda?

What the children are really talking about when they share with us their sliding spectrum of humanity is what I would call *botheredness*. The act of botheredness is essential in motivating and engaging children. I suppose botheredness actually sums the following up quite neatly.

 **Positive teacher acts**

1 Smiling

2 Laughter

3 Encouragement

4 Praise

5 Time

(I love it when an acronym emerges ...)

These may seem a bit cuddly and fluffy to you but the truth is this: *these are essential teacher acts* in the world of engagement. This is the *tough stuff*, not the fluffy stuff. You can have all the knowledge in the world around your subject but if you cannot connect on a human level with children then maybe teaching isn't the job for you. If you feel a little cynicism towards this humble list, then imagine the opposites.

 **Awful teacher acts**

1 Grimacing

2 Shouting

3 Humiliation

4 Punishment

5 3 o'clock merchant – specifically, the act of legging it home bang on three o'clock

Where are you in terms of positive teacher acts? Place yourself on this scale by drawing a line on the spectrum.

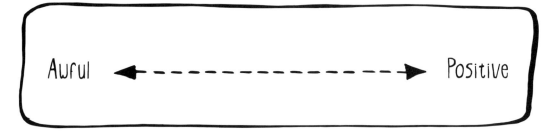

These positive teacher acts can be defined like this:

Smile

When I work with groups of newly qualified teachers (NQTs) I always like to ask if any of them have been advised to 'not smile until Christmas'. To my amazement, many still put up their hands. A brief discussion ensues and we quickly realise that this particular pearl of wisdom is limp, lame and the ultimate in weak engagement strategies. One of the greatest tools in our *teacher armoury* is our ability to smile. Children are drawn into the safety and warmth of a smile; they can be disarmed by it. 'A smile confuses an approaching frown', the saying goes. And it's true. The great thing is you (hopefully) don't have to go on a course to learn about smiling and it's the easiest addition to a teacher's *human armoury* – that invisible sack that every professional walks about with, adding to at every opportunity.

Amazingly some newly qualified teachers say they've been advised to 'not smile until Christmas'. A brief discussion ensues and we quickly realise that this particular pearl of wisdom is limp, lame and the ultimate in weak engagement strategies. One of the greatest tools in our teacher armoury is our ability to smile.

Laughter

This is a tough one. Especially with tough classes. Children can sometimes take a joke too far, but if you've worked on your expectations and relationships in the room, then the boundaries should be clear. Laughing with children demonstrates that you are sharing an experience with them – it puts you all in the same place. It shows that you are human.

Encouragement

This is a key engagement tool. Put another way, it's *talking to children about their work*. Highlighting the good, reflecting on work that has been done before and outlining the simplest and most direct routes to improvement are the ingredients of an encouraging conversation. This isn't rocket science, but I know some teachers who just don't talk to kids at all. Funnily enough, they have more negative relationships with their pupils than others.

Praise

Praise ties in closely with encouragement of course. Praise can be a comment to an individual, a class or the whole school during assembly. Praise can also manifest itself in celebrations of great work. A display can demonstrate praise (e.g. Worker of the Week). Praise is different from *reward* although children don't really distinguish between the two. A smiley sticker at the end of a piece of work or a postcard home outlining a child's success constitutes worthy praise, and offers a reward in the form of a tangible gift.

Time

There is no such thing as a teacher with time on their hands. Time is the biggest block to everything teachers want to do. However, if you demonstrate that you have time to children, they will appreciate it; perhaps not straight away – maybe in twenty years or so. A few years ago there was a government advertising campaign for teacher recruitment that had the tag line

---

Everyone remembers a good teacher.

Do you remember it? More importantly, do *you* remember a good teacher? Think about it now. I recollect John Booth at my secondary school. He was a Maths teacher and a head of year. He never actually taught me formally – I just know for certain that he was *bothered*. He ran trips, attended concerts and did the whole deal. When I went to pick up my disappointing exam results, he took me to his office and talked me through my options. It was his summer holiday. When I remember a good teacher, I think of him because he exuded

Botheredness.

It's the same for you too, isn't it? The good teachers we remember are the ones who were able to make it look like they had time; the ones who could smile, laugh, encourage and praise. I remember the bad teachers as well. Do you? What were their awful traits?

So where do you place yourself? What kind of teacher are you? What kind of teacher do you want to be? Have you got *the human app*?

Just a thought: What about them kids?

 **Kid types**

1 **Geek:** This child knows lots about stuff that they really shouldn't know at their age. Like exhaustive knowledge of 1960s TV show *The Prisoner* or fossils. They also relate everything you attempt to teach them to their particular geek-focus.

For example:

Teacher: Today we are looking at estuaries.

Geek Kid: Great! Portmeirion in North Wales is built on an estuary and that's where they filmed *The Prisoner*! There's also a delightful array of pottery on display there!

These sorts of kids can really wind you up and you will think of them consistently as you plan lessons. Eventually you will start tailoring some of the learning of the whole class around the geek's main interests. And that's scary. I know, I've done it.

2   **Emo/Goth:** A massively misunderstood group, and indeed diverse, as described in this anonymous ditty I discovered online:

The Difference between Emo and Goth:
Emos hate themselves
Goths hate everyone
Emos want to kill themselves
Goths want to kill everyone

Don't try to understand it, just accept it. These kids want to stand out yet at the same time they don't want the spotlight on them. They love the world but aren't that keen on the people who run it. The good news is that, more often than not, they are not as scary as they look.

3   **Genius:** The bane of every teacher's life – often referred to as *gifted and talented* – the pupil who is so bright they are causing light pollution in the middle of the day. This kid is different from the geek because s/he knows lots about everything. It's the type of child who can:

- Finish sentences for you

- Predict your next learning move during a lesson

- Be extremely practical and creative

- Chatter to the point that they can offer a kind of DVD commentary to your lesson

- Scare you with their intelligence

4   **Passenger/Grey:** This is the child who you sense has an internal monologue going on which is basically dissecting every aspect of you – your professionalism, your resource choices – whilst you deliver your lesson. Not that scary as they tend to do everything you ask of them. Which is a good job, because if one of these kids suddenly kicked off in your lesson, it'd become the talk of the school. And your reputation would crumble.

5   **Adventurer:** This is the type of child who really used to come into their own when on a school trip. (Remember them – school trips?) This child is fearless; the one who would happily leap over a dry stone wall without checking if there was a five metre drop on the other side. Relentlessly enthusiastic outside the classroom. And that's scary.

6   **Flexible:** This child sounds perfect for your classroom but can challenge you in terms of their innate ability to turn their hand to anything you put in front of them. When things don't go their way, they may be mildly upset, but deal with it. This is the kid who doesn't freak out when there is a room change or suddenly turn into Satan because a supply teacher is taking your lesson. They essentially handle things better than a lot of adults would. And that of course is scary.

7   **Fearful:** Pretty much the opposite of number 6. Cry a lot. Bit like you on a Sunday night.

8   **Feisty:** These types have the tendency to have a negative persistence and will go on and on nagging, whining and negotiating if there is something they particularly want. Like a dog with a bone, these kids want consistency on their terms. You better warn them if you're trying a new approach or are changing rooms for the day. Also if you are changing your haircut.

9 **Gangsta:** A child who thinks they are from South Central Los Angeles. But actually they're from Chorley. If you show them *respeck*, you may well get it back. My most recent Gangstas were an absolute joy, but when they walked into the room for the first time I was, admittedly, filled with dread.

10 **Rebel (without a clue):** This child is your classic case of basically being contrary just for the sake of it. This is the kind of rebel who, if you ask them, 'If little Tommy jumped into a burning building, would you?' will answer in the affirmative. If you suggest Shakespeare never published any of his plays, the rebel will ask you how you know. The rebel hates school but comes every day, hates teachers but wants them to listen, and is *well street* but doesn't know who the prime minister is. Rebels are often likeable, which is also scary.

This is the really scary bit however:

All of these children are our responsibility.

And that is something we have to come to terms with as soon as we enter the teaching profession. Whether they are 3 years old or 15, when they are in our classrooms we have to do the best we can for them. Even if they're frightening.

Now, these kid types are what they are: absolute stereotypes. And, of course, stereotypes aren't real. Sort of. The children who are real are the ones in your classroom, the ones working hard to improve their results, the ones staring out of the window because they're not interested in what you're teaching them because, to paraphrase Morrissey, it says nothing to them about their lives.

We work with real kids

The real kids are the ones we meet every day – not just the children who are captured on mobile devices plundering shops for the latest trainers. We work with the children who:

• Hold a door open for you on the main corridor

• Nod at you because you also have a season ticket

• Occasionally look at you like you're from Mars

• Want to please

- Want you to do all the work in maintaining the positive teacher–pupil relationship

- See school as a chore (SCHOOL = Seven Crappy Hours Of Our Lives)

- Have zero support from home

- Feel safe when they're with us

- Live in poverty

- Are street-wise because they have to be

It might not say 'miracle worker' on your job description but frankly, some of the time at least, that's what you are. Particularly in this age of external bureaucracy, analysis, competition and educational experts.

Ah. Educational experts. I'm not thinking of the genuine people who perhaps support your school from time to time. I'm thinking of some of the voices you may hear on the radio or the folk who pop up being all expert on *Newsnight*. Let's have a moment ...

A word on educational experts
I probably don't need to tell you this, but if there are experts appearing on the radio or television spouting on about education then you need to give them a credibility litmus test. Basically, if they've never taught in a classroom on a wet November afternoon, then *they fail*. Listen to them by all means, but add a pinch of salt. Here are some examples of *experts*:

- **Greying academics:** I've no problem at all with academics or people who are grey – indeed, I resemble George Clooney (only) in the hair department more day by day. I just don't want to know what your view is of young people if the last time you spoke to one was in Oxford in 1968.

- **Failed teachers:** Tried teaching for three weeks having scraped through a teacher training course, got taken to the cleaners by the children, now ubiquitous in the media slagging off schools which put children at the centre of everything they do, often in difficult circumstances. Essentially, failed teachers give teachers a bad name.

- **Politicians:** Bless 'em. They mean well but spend too much time listening to the above. Alternatively, they're a bunch of overzealous, ladder-climbing, educationally naive 20-somethings who feel that because they once wrote a paper for a think tank they can now help set government policy. But don't get me started ...

MPs, commentators,
failed teachers,
think tanks

66%

Parents (people who went
to school recently)

28%

Teachers and children

6%

Who does the world listen to
in matters of education?

- **Grown-ups:** Some adults have been scarred by their schooling. So, naturally, they hate schools and think schools do a terrible job and essentially lie at the root of all that is wrong with kids today. This group of adults left school way back in 1981 with a clutch of qualifications. They still, however, see themselves as experts and view education through that lens. Other adults are in awe of you if you work in education. My brother is like that. He works in a popular department store and believes that teachers should be given danger money. He left school in 1983 and remembers his teachers fondly. Bottom line: Everyone went to school = everyone's an expert = we have to accept this.

- **Parents:** See above. I remember a parent telling me I was *paid* to make her son behave in my class – the boy was very challenging and a nasty piece of work in many respects. The parent basically absolved herself of all responsibility for him once he left her sight in the morning. Other parents are absolutely fantastic and I could fill this book with great stories about them and how I have felt supported and appreciated by them. Set up a class blog for your class and invite parents to contribute – it really will encourage you. Better still, if you are a parent, make sure you do your bit and contribute in whatever way you can to your child's school.

The best way of establishing if it is worth listening to an educational expert is to imagine them delivering a lesson to the most difficult class you've ever had (13- and 14-year-olds in my English class, Wakefield 1993–1994 works for me every time). Could they hack it personally and would what they're saying help? Yes or no. Easy really.

And remember, being with an expert who you think has something to say doesn't make you a bad teacher. Quite the opposite.

Tell-tale signs that you are a good teacher

1   You get very excited in stationery shops

2   You enjoy Friday nights

3   You think carefully about your hairstyle

4   Being paid overtime is an alien concept

5   You can converse with children

6 Your car boot resembles a stock cupboard

7 You've got metaphorical wing mirrors attached to your head so that you can look back, reflect, learn and be a better teacher

8 You are confident in what you do

9 You're happy to take some risks

10 You ask for glove puppets for Christmas

A word or two on drains and radiators

Drains

These are the colleagues who turn up to work, do the job and then leave. Devoid of botheredness. When I first started teaching I sat in the staffroom with a group of drains. By half term I was slagging off the kids, trying to leg it out of the door at the end of the day like a proper 3 o'clock merchant and wholly disinterested in the young people I was working with. However, I came to my senses because I realised I was growing to hate work, was really cynical about leadership decisions and didn't like my classes. I knew this wasn't normal for an NQT, so I did something quite radical: *I sat somewhere else*. And that was it. Fortunately, this sort of teacher is becoming hard to find (you can judge this by looking at your colleagues in school). The opposite of a drain? A radiator, of course.

Radiators

These are the colleagues you aspire to be like; the colleagues who get things done and don't bang on about it. These teachers exude botheredness, warmth and generosity of spirit. They are fun to be around and you learn from them. I could write a list of the radiators I know. Can you?

So, where are you on this scale? Where do you want to be? What do you need to do to get there?

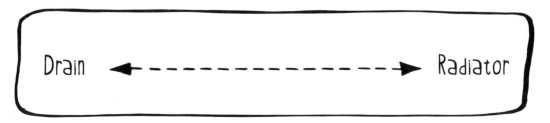

Features of radiators

- **Patience:** Every teacher needs this. Even when you're standing in front of a class and you're biting your tongue and clenching your fists. You still need patience. When the child is simply not getting it – the equation, the poetic meaning, the scientific conclusion – you need to persist. The ability to *hold time*, to wait and to give opportunity for thinking is essential to engagement. We always say that we don't have enough time (see above; but then you don't have time to go back do you – sorry) but we can show children that we can *give time* by planning our lessons carefully and factoring in these waiting moments. The children will see this as *patience*.

- **Moral purpose:** This is the reason you get out of bed. As well as for the holidays and the money.

- **A growth mindset:** This is the drive that keeps you motivated and makes you want to keep improving. Schools should operate clear and thorough appraisal processes that allow you to target the particular aspects of your practice you wish to develop. It used to be called performance management. What does this look like in your school? How are *you* encouraged and expected to grow? What are you learning whilst teaching?

At a school I used to work in, there was a group of us who wanted the opportunity to work closer together. So we set up our own mini-Insets every Monday night. Each week a different member of the group would lead the hour long session. NQTs, trainees, heads of department and the school leadership team were invited. From this humble beginning, I learned absolutely loads from my colleagues, especially around the subject of technology. Today, this sort of session has evolved into a TeachMeet. If you haven't been to one, go; if you can't find one, organise one for your area. Basically teachers from all walks of life (from trainees to head teachers) are invited to present to each other. When not presenting, we are *lurking*.

These presentations take two forms:

» Micro-presentation usually lasting seven minutes where the teacher presents something they (or a colleague) have done in class. It could be a list of strategies, a resource or a scheme of work. What it can't be is an untested idea. Or a sales pitch.

» Nano-presentation usually lasting up to two minutes.

A TeachMeet I went to recently had a healthy mix of new technology, posters and singing. Yes, singing. If you want to know more about TeachMeets, some are listed in the *Times Educational Supplement* on a Friday but perhaps the best source is on Twitter using the hashtag #teachmeet. If this last sentence made absolutely no sense to you whatsoever, keep reading, and when you've finished the book, get on the Internet.

- **Emotional intelligence:** See the list of 'Ten things not to say in a staffroom' below. EI (or EQ if you prefer) was a bit of a buzzphrase a few years back. That shouldn't trivialise it though. If you want to engage children and colleagues, you will need EI. You have good emotional intelligence if you can:

  » Demonstrate empathy

  » Listen well

  » Control your emotions

  » Understand the makeup of the school you work in – its positive and negative aspects

  For more on EI, seek out Daniel Goleman's book *Emotional Intelligence: Why It Can Matter More than IQ.*

- **The ability to help people shine:** This isn't me going all fluffy again. I suppose this is the daddy of this list. If we can help children (and our colleagues) achieve their potential by engaging them in meaningful activity, then they will shine. How do we do this? Well hopefully, this book will help you.

 Things not to say in a staffroom

1 I just got another outstanding!

2 That Inset day was hopeless (unless of course it was)

3 I'm getting off early today

4 I'm still a bit tiddly

5 I can't be bothered with SEN – too much hassle

6 I know the kids like your subject, but it's not as important as the core subjects, is it?

7 I put in the winning bid on eBay whilst my kids were working

8   This school is shit

9   You can't make a silk purse out of a sow's ear

10 My goodness. I think I've won the Lottery!

 Teacher types you'll find in any staffroom

1   **Rose tinted:** As in 'It was never like this at my last school'

2   **Never any trouble for me:** As in 'History class? Trouble? They were great for me last year!'

3   **Terrorist:** Who sits with other terrorists in training events and meetings taking pot-shots from afar but never actually does anything

4   **Mutterer:** Who mutters stuff to themselves in reaction to new initiatives

5   **Supply:** A fed-up teacher who is constantly in a rush. Spends a lot of the day waiting for work to be delivered to the class they're covering. Used to teach woodwork. Carries a newspaper and a coffee everywhere

6   **Job seeker:** Spends every available moment leafing through teaching jobs. Doesn't get the hint when even the head points out opportunities in other schools

7   **Trainee:** Shell-shocked and usually seen carrying large files

8   **Is it on the trolley?** Usually to be found around the kitchen area of the staffroom. Baking cakes and complaining about the washing-up a speciality. Microwaves kippers

9   **Dame:** The drama queen, male or female. Rarely Drama teachers. They work harder than everyone else apparently. When asked to do something, they throw their hands into the air and start speaking very loudly about time and workload

10 **You:** Where do you fit in?

Here's another way of looking at it. Which quadrant do you see yourself in?

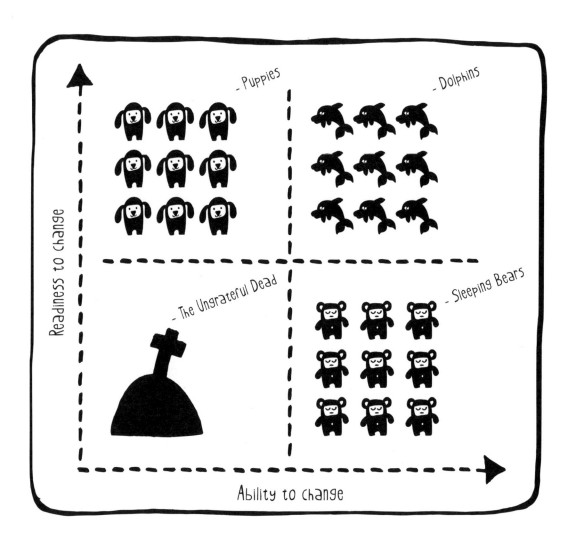

So where do you place yourself? Here are some explanations to help you along:

- **Dolphins:** Teachers who take risks, share, demonstrate the positive teacher acts described above and seek to take others with them. They have the ability and readiness to embrace change

- **Puppies:** NQTs, recently qualified teachers and other professionals who simply need confidence and guidance from the Dolphins to change and develop

- **Sleeping Bears:** Teachers who are brilliant but may be sitting in the wrong part of the staffroom; those who have forgotten their own potential. Can be grumpy

- **The Ungrateful Dead:** See 'Drains' earlier in this chapter. Neither willing nor able

The very fact that you're reading this book means you must have stumbled away from the Ungrateful Dead quadrant at least, so well done. If you've found out where you are, now place your colleagues. Don't tell them. Just do it in your head. Interesting, isn't it!

Back to the human app

What is your unique selling point (USP)? I know you're not a shampoo or new flavour of crisp. But if you were, how would you market yourself? If you had to 'sell' your *teacherhood*, what would make you stand out from the crowd?

Get a piece of paper and write down your unique selling points. If you're a Language teacher, you've got a USP straight away. If you're an NQT, then you've hopefully got lots of innovative ideas (as well as fresh enthusiasm) to sell. If you're a leader, what makes you a *great* leader? Honestly, grab that paper and get cracking. Are you a *shadow* (Hank Marvin) or a *face* (Rod Stewart)?

Here's one I made earlier:

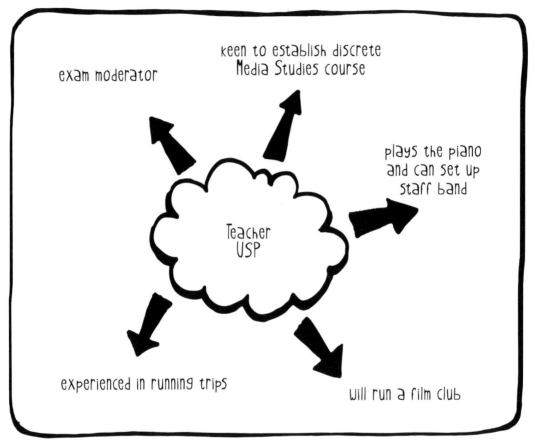

A question I've asked when interviewing prospective candidates for teaching posts is: 'What are you bringing to the school?' In other words, what makes you unique? This is particularly important if the job market is swamped with potential applicants. Whatever you do, find your USP. You'll notice my example above doesn't really have a lot to do with the classroom and what goes on in it. The reason for this is that for really fantastic engagement inside the classroom you have to ensure things are right outside it. That way, people will let you get on with it. They'll trust your judgement and understand the creative risks you want to take with your children in your classroom.

Five other things to think about

1   Begin developing a professional learning network (PLN). If you get on Twitter or attend (or indeed, organise) a TeachMeet, this will start to happen quicker than you think. A PLN is basically a group of teachers who get together and whom you can call upon if you need professional support (e.g. teaching ideas!)

2   Consider the times when you have learned. When did it happen? What did you learn? Why was it memorable?

3   Don't stand around waiting for opportunities to open themselves up to you. You may well be surprised at how much can change for the better as the result of an *honest conversation*

4   Offer to do stuff for your school. You'd want your own child's teachers to do it, so what's stopping you? Step up and be a face, not a shadow

5   If everything is as good as it can be outside of the classroom, you'll have more room for manoeuvre within it

The one last element of the human app is something called *unconditional positive regard*. A term coined by psychologist Carl Rogers, unconditional positive regard is the basic acceptance of a person regardless of that person's actions. In the teaching context of course we're talking about children. As teachers, children need to feel safe with us – even if they sometimes seem scary! If a child tells you to f*** off on Monday, there's no point in holding a grudge against them for the rest of the week. You're allowed to be upset by it, of course, but keep it inside; let the sanctions and punishments take place and then *move on*. It's sad to hear teachers say things like:

Those kids will never learn
or
I don't see why I have to teach her. She's awful.

If we can operate as teachers with unconditional positive regard for our children, then we see them as the most important element of what we do – the centre of our practice. That's how it should be, shouldn't it?

Unconditional positive regard is actually very liberating: it helps keep the activity and work in your classroom moving. Whether you are planning a trip to another galaxy, plotting out supply runs in the trenches or writing a shopping list for the BFG from Roald Dahl's story, keeping the children with you is vital – this engagement, and the willingness from the children to *be engaged*, lies at the heart of creative classroom practice. If we can model this approach to children – and to colleagues – we may go some way in actually making a difference beyond the classroom. Whenever things go awry in society, schools get the blame early doors. As a humble teacher in your humble classroom though, you really do have the power to change the lives of the children in your care. If only for a few hours.

Now get ready for a curriculum overhaul ...

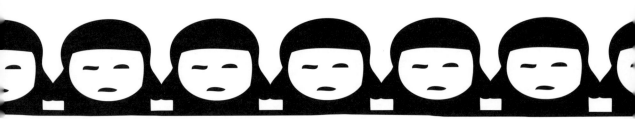

- STand out from the team

OR Inventing a Curriculum Inside Your Classroom ...

OR A Curriculum Worth Engaging In
(and lessons worth behaving for) ...

OR We're Gonna Need a Bigger Boat

Liberating Your Subject

Luck is when preparation meets opportunity.

Seneca, Roman dramatist, ages ago

 Things that keep me awake at night

1 Changes and innovations in technology

2 Hitting my forties

3 Gaps in my knowledge of everything

4 The mortgage

5 The unreliability of sat nav

6 My lapses in confidence

7 Deadlines

8 Unmade films that play in my head

9 Wasted opportunities

10 The preciousness of Time

Other things that keep me awake at night

1 Building tunnels through mountains

2 Touch-button time travel

3 How to liberate and celebrate a gorgon

4 Being homeless

5 Organising a carnival in a grumpy farmer's field

6 Decorating the castle ready for the arrival of the king

7 Evicting the old man from the house he has lived in all his life

8 Preparing Beowulf's armour and weaponry

9 Getting those bats out of the attic

10 The nature of bravery

I used to think that being *innovative* and *engaging* in the classroom meant being at the cutting edge of everything, totally up to speed with technology and basically existing as an all-round living and breathing educational guru. I've since realised it's none of these things. It's good to be up to date, to have some knowledge of current educational debates and to understand the true meanings of the educational buzzwords that drift in and out of fashion. You can do all of these things by following a few decent contributors to Twitter or by reading the *Times Educational Supplement* on a Friday. Being innovative and engaging in a classroom actually comes down to *you* and what it is you want to teach. Consider this: you may have a head of department who hands you the schemes of work in August and says:

I've written these for this year. Enjoy!

You are left standing holding a load of paper that is essentially your instruction manual for the year. Part of you may feel like this is a fantastic turn of events, as you were expecting to have to write them yourself and really were leaving it to the last minute. But now, problem solved: winner!

Step back a minute though. Have a think about it. It really isn't a winner moment at all, is it? Someone – your superior – is basically treating you like a monkey. And because you're instantly gratified at the revelation that you've got little planning to do, all of a sudden, you're smiling like one. It's all a bit fast-food-kebab: initially feels great, and then, a little later, makes you a bit sick. Secondary colleagues need to spare a thought for primary colleagues at times like this. I couldn't believe it when my primary teacher mate told me he had to hand his planning in weekly to his head teacher. This essentially wrecked his Sundays as he frantically prepared everything to deliver to his head each Monday morning. What a total nightmare. In secondary schools we have a melt-down-freak-out and think about getting the union reps in when asked to supply individual lesson plans as part of observation processes. We really need to get a grip.

Things that keep a head of department awake at night

1 Data

2 Exam entries

3 Loose cannon colleague

4 Subject credibility

5 Inspection

6 Does the head like me?

7 Disappointing appointment to the team

8 The second in department

9 Marking

10 Where do I go next with my so-called career?

So, your head of department has done all the work for you. This essentially means that:

- You have been robbed of stamping your mark on anything fresh in the schemes of work for a whole year

- Boundaries have been erected around the work you can do with your kids in the form of someone else's learning outcomes

- You will be delivering someone else's learning formula – a little like opening a franchise, but unlike Subway, you won't make any profit

- You are a monkey. A puppet. A monkey puppet

If you're an NQT or someone hungry for new ideas, then the thought of being given the schemes of work for a full academic year *is* ace! No question about it. However, you still need the opportunity to make the teaching and learning *yours* in your classroom. Have ownership over it. The trouble with prescriptive plans is that they assume outcomes along predicted routes. What they don't always account for is the unknown, the what if and the unpredictable. Only you can do that. So when your head of department says:

I've written these for this year. Enjoy!

You need to reply with:

Fantastic. I'm really grateful. I'm going to add some stuff of my own as well if that's okay. I really want to contribute. Can I meet with you and tell you some of my ideas?

Your head of department will appreciate this because they've not been sleeping well. If you are clear that you will be trying some of your own ideas in the classroom, this will be well received *as long as you have worked on your credibility* – are you a shadow or a face?

When I became a head of department I thought it was my responsibility to write all the schemes of work and basically direct my entire team with what I wanted them to teach. This meant that I had to transplant my teaching persona into a Word document, ensure we hit all the things that we should be doing whilst also remaining a department of innovation. I essentially created a dictatorship, and it was a big mistake. The same year, I had appointed two very good NQTs. By handing them my document, I stifled their ideas and innovation – part of the reason I wanted bloomin' NQTs in the first place!

Fortunately, halfway through the year, one of the NQTs came to me and asked if she could contribute some new projects to the established scheme of work.

This is how I reacted *in my head*:

- Who the hell do you think you are?
- I think you're getting a bit too big for your boots, young lady
- Are you saying mine are crap?
- Do you think you're better than me?
- You think I'm rubbish don't you?
- You don't realise that I lie awake at night worrying about all sorts of things (see above list)

What I *actually said* was:

Of course you can. Absolutely. What are you thinking?

And so a really good conversation ensued. This NQT had done it right. Before long I'd pretty much binned many of my (tried and tested) schemes of work and our team was actually having *useful* meetings establishing the focus of our new projects. Each member of the team (there were four of us) then took responsibility for the creation and resourcing of a project. This might not sound like rocket science to you, but this was team innovation in action in my school!

The new projects had a fresh slant on them – this was my stipulation in giving my colleagues free rein: the new 'slant' was that I wanted the children to take more ownership over the direction of their learning. I wanted our team to set up projects (inspired by what happens in primary schools) that enabled our pupils to negotiate their way through a topic *guided* by the teacher, rather than just be set tasks that would be performed and assessed at the end of the half term.

I wanted my staff to take these risks:

- Walk into the room without really knowing where the session was going to go – don't panic. I mean this figuratively; of course they knew where the session was going to go, it's just that other things might emerge during the session that would be far more interesting than what the teacher had planned

- Ask very open questions that would challenge the children

- Give children decisions to make

- Be the guide on the side, not the sage on the stage

- Follow the elephant outside the classroom (more of this later)

- Step back and allow the children to resolve dilemmas

- Throw real-life scenarios at the class and see how they deal with it (e.g. How should we deal with looters? How can we help child soldiers in Somalia?)

- Broaden their subject experience by taking on more specialist areas within Drama (in this case, mask work and Mantle of the Expert (see Chapter 1))

- Use technology to capture and playback work. We used Flip cameras back in the day and today image capture technology is commonplace in schools. At this time, they were cutting edge and an absolute gift to teachers of more practical subjects
- Stop 'making up plays' and actually use Drama as an exploratory tool of learning (this *was* Drama)

A word about Drama

Please bear in mind that as I write this, I love Drama. You might not. That's fine. This isn't a book about Drama. I'm just going to write about what I believe people's perceptions are of my subject. Why don't you set up a blog and write down what *you* think people think about the subject you're closest to? Teachers are doing this all over the world and are actually connecting with each other. Try www.posterous.com or www.blogger.com to get you going!

Drama myths

- Drama classes are full of middle-class kids doing plays set in mental homes where the pinnacle of great performance is some girl running around, wide-eyed and chanting. Guaranteed A*
- Drama is just a timetabled *Glee* club where children can express themselves through voice, body and movement
- No deep, rigorous study exists
- Drama teachers are all over-passionate luvvie-types who don't write their reports properly
- Drama is about making up plays. That's it
- It's a bit *gay*. No! Hold on! When I went through my Advanced Skills Teacher assessment, the external assessor actually said that to me! I couldn't believe it. Neither could the head

Try and get *your* subject myths together. Are any of the following true?

- Geography is just about maps
- Science is doing experiments and setting fire to your mate's hair
- History is about old stuff

- Literacy is about writing things

- Phonics is a form of slow-motion break-dancing

- English is about reading out loud and being humiliated

- Maths is just about numbers and stuff that will be totally useless in your life. Like algebra

- Music is only good if your parents get you learning an instrument

- PE is running about being shouted at by a man in a shell suit

Let's face it, Drama has always been seen as a Mickey Mouse subject. If you get a qualification in Drama, it proves that you are versatile, confident and imaginative. If it's the *only* qualification you get, however, it just shows how bloody easy it is. Apparently. Drama operates on a no-win scenario and has done for years. The way it is assessed in a lot of schools reflects the way it has been valued by successive governments. Everyone loves a good school play/show/musical. It's absolutely fantastic public relations for the school and, for secondaries in particular, it's a great way of getting parents into the building.

In terms of timetabling and rooming, the subject always comes a cropper. I've taught in dining rooms (complete with sausage roll skids on the floor), libraries, Science labs (seriously) and outside. In the drizzle. Drama's always been the ugly stepchild of English and schools are full of English teachers 'doing' Drama when they are actually far from qualified to do so. They once went on an Inset course to do Drama Techniques. It's a bit like me teaching Dance because I can throw some shapes after a few glasses of wine. Or teaching German because I like *Kelly's Heroes*. The sad thing is, there are some Drama teachers who are quite content with projecting this unreality around the subject – in the same way that there are some PE teachers who just want to have a kick about, and some Food Technologists who just bake scones all day. And microwave kippers. This government – indeed any government – isn't interested in Drama in school. Never has been. And yet, they are really missing a trick.

Reasons why Drama isn't fluffy nonsense, *Glee* club and making up plays

1 Drama can stimulate creativity in problem-solving

2 Drama can challenge young people's perceptions about the world and their place in it

3 Drama allows young people to explore real situations from a variety of points of view and in a safe environment

4 Drama provides training for all aspects of human communication

5 Drama reinforces tolerance, compromise and empathy

6 Drama develops self-control and discipline

7 Drama is absolutely team-orientated

8 Drama reinforces and supports the rest of the school curriculum

9 Drama helps children develop confidence and self-esteem

10 Drama always takes place in the present; therefore it is always relevant

Right, get your pen and write down what's so bloody special about your subject/specialist area! Why do this?

Because:

• You have a passion for your subject or specialist area

• You're the expert

• You know how to 'sell' your passion to kids

• It's cathartic!

• Bottom line: if you're engaged with your stuff, then you should be able to engage the kids

Why bother?

If you can stand up for your subject (don't forget, we all have to stand up for our subjects at one point or another) then we are demonstrating a real commitment to it, to our practice and to the kids in our classes.

If you're a primary teacher reading this and you're thinking 'I teach loads of subjects, what's this got to do with me?' then please consider some of the subject areas at risk in the primary curriculum. For example, in your school, who is responsible for the delivery of Physical Education, Drama or Music? More and more primary schools are getting in outside providers to deliver these (and other) subject areas whilst the regular class teacher has their planning, preparation and assessment time (PPA). Don't get me wrong – you need your PPA! However, how do the children you teach regard the subjects you're not teaching? Do they see them as a *treat*? As a *reward*? Or do they see them as *not as important* as the stuff you teach because, basically, you don't teach it to them? It's like the school piano. If no one can play, then it simply gets used as a bookshelf. It's just something to think about ...

No matter how old the children you teach, there's one thing for sure: *the curriculum you deliver needs to make sense*. Children and young people don't have (and don't want) access to your schemes of work. What you *say* is what they *get*. I did a whole school training day recently and the head teacher asked if we could start a little later than planned because the teachers needed more time to get their worksheets prepared for the following day. I'm not going to get trapped into banging on about worksheets, but the point is that as a consequence of the head saying that, I got this impression of the school (which I'd been standing in for only seven minutes):

- The children were passive

- The teachers lacked imagination

- The teachers lacked creativity

- The curriculum belonged to no one

- Learning was task driven

I also learned that I sometimes jump to conclusions – as the staff were all very nice. They weren't buzzing though, and that's a prerequisite for any engaging teacher. Isn't it? A diet consisting of endless streams of worksheets isn't good for anyone. Ironically, it slows the hunger for knowledge and encourages children to disengage and to do the minimum. As long as the sheet is completed, job done. *Really*?

Worksheet spectrum – where are you?

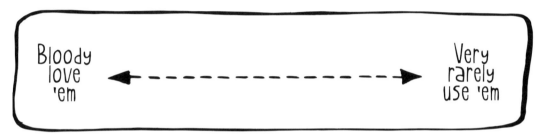

Over-reliance on worksheets and textbooks can interrupt the coherent nature of a really good sequence of learning. Rather than deepen understanding, they can confuse, distract and vandalise understanding. Scoping in on your core business of teaching, I offer you RAVE as a way of looking at your coherent schemes of work and your curriculum in your classroom:

Relevant: e.g. a curriculum that enables pupils to see the real world outside the classroom whilst supporting their ethical and moral development

Academic: e.g. the facts and the knowledge around specific subjects and themes

Vocational: e.g. adopting practical skills and procedures to real tasks whilst developing expertise

Evaluation: e.g. Assessment for Learning, Assessment of Learning

In the interest of creativity, I'll discuss these four elements in reverse order, so I'll start with evaluation.

Evaluation

We often think that evaluation should happen at the end of something. It's like the full point at the end of a piece of writing. To me, evaluation is something that is ongoing. Inspectors agree, except they call it the *mini-plenary*! Evaluation can be formal, like a test or exam, but it doesn't have to be. Evaluation can be two children discussing each other's work in progress. Evaluation could be seen as the experience of listening to another talk about your work. Evaluation can be a teacher's encouraging comment. Evaluation can also be a reflective comment written by a child to the teacher on a sticky note stuck on the wall at the end of a lesson. Worksheets don't provide this dialogue. Evaluation is so much more than 'This is what I did today and this is how I think I did'.

Vocational

When do we teach compromise? When do we teach active listening? Or creativity? For me, the word *vocational* conjures up images of visiting speakers, unused university prospectuses and work experience (where I would usually get to visit a large number of beauty salons). Yet vocational learning to me, although connected to all of this, is also a million miles from it. We start vocational training in the early years when, hopefully building on what has been learned in the home, we teach sharing, caring, boundaries and listening, amongst other things, through the vehicle of play. In primary classrooms we see the tables arranged in ways that are conducive to group work (cabaret or café style) – children can work individually, in pairs or in groups of three or four with such arrangements. In secondary schools we have, in recent years, had the Personal, Learning and Thinking Skills (PLTS, or sometimes called Plerts, Pluts or Pelts) which attempted (successfully in my opinion) to rationalise learner attributes that would be useful for progress, for success and for the future. Broken down, the PLTS looked like this:

- Independent enquirers
- Creative thinkers
- Reflective learners
- Team workers
- Self-managers
- Effective participants

It appears the PLTS have fallen out of favour with current educational policy makers with their focus on a fact-based curriculum rather than one that cultivates abstract thinking skills and problem-solving. As a statement of intent, I think the PLTS provide us with an excellent benchmark for what we need to be delivering to our children. Look at the list this way:

I want the children in my class to be independent enquirers, creative thinkers, reflective learners, team workers, self-managers and effective participants.

In other words, children in my class will ask great questions, think about solutions, ponder on how as well as what they have learned, participate positively in groups, remember to bring a pen and join in. Essentially, the PLTS offered us a cool list of attributes we would want from anyone – from schoolchildren to leaders of industry. Speaking of leaders of industry, there's always a few of them knocking around on the television complaining that schools don't provide an able workforce with the ability to do a good job. I think they're wrong. However, I do believe that we sometimes prepare children for the life of work a little too late. By lacing the PLTS, or our own version of them, into our teaching we may be able to do something about this and stem the criticism that's always thrown at us.

Academic

Or, as taxi drivers would say, The Knowledge. Interestingly, the word *academic* can also be defined as meaning 'having no practical purpose or use'. I like that. Academic, the noun, also conjures up images of ancient people in dusty rooms surrounded by decaying leather-bound libraries. For us, of course, it's the content. The stuff we want to deliver. The pedagogy is *how* we are going to that. This is hopefully why you're reading this book.

Relevant

This is the important one for me (and it should be for you), so I'm going to write it in bigger blummin' letters:

Relevant

I suppose this is the bit that makes school matter to children. To paraphrase Morrissey again, school has to *say something to me about my life*. Your classroom and the teaching and learning that happen within it needs to make sense to the children – it should be relevant and humanising. This isn't just a pseudo personal and social education add-on, this is ensuring that your content makes *learning sense* and is actually resonating with the children you are teaching. Don't forget, this applies from the youngest of our children upwards. If they are gripped by the academic, then it's because they see it as relevant to them. This is the eternal struggle for teachers – getting the content to be attractive to the learner. This is what engagement is: the successful 'selling' of the academic; and my advice to you is to make it as relevant as you can.

How?

 Things you can do to make your lessons relevant

1 Know your children

2 Know the community where you teach and they live

3 Know what's going on in the world and see the learning potential in it

4 Stop rehashing old projects

5 Give way to your crazier ideas

6 Stop blaming lack of experimentation, risk and innovation on your lack of *time*

7 See your children as future adults – prepare them for the world

8 Keep your lesson content flexible

9 Make your learning and teaching *pro-social*

10 Burn your worksheets

Things not to ignore when thinking about relevance

1 The core industry (if there's one left) of your community

2 Where the school community sits geographically (e.g. coastal, rural, urban)

3 The news – local, national and international

4 What children are talking about

5 The future of the school

If the content is relevant, you may have to work quite hard to make it dull.

Here's an example of some work I did in a rural community school just before Bonfire Night. I'm not writing a lesson plan here, I just want to tell you what happened. Whilst you're reading it, ask yourself how this is relevant to the learners, what they are learning and how it ties into the RAVE curriculum highlighted above.

Rural community school just before Bonfire Night

Resources: A letter from the council, large sheets of paper, fat pens, a pair of wellies, sticky notes

Class: Twenty-eight bubbly 7-year-olds who have been learning about hedgerows (many of the children come from farming families)

With the children in a circle the teacher *paints* the scene: a field surrounded by hedgerows. The classroom floor is the field and its walls are the hedges. The teacher points out where the gate providing an exit from the field is located.

Build on the painted scene by asking *sensory questions* such as: What do we feel underfoot? Is there a breeze? What do we see beyond the field?

We focus on the hedges. Building on prior learning, we talk about what animals might live in these hedges. We write the suggestions on sticky notes and put them around the classroom – under the bookshelves, above the Health and Safety notice, next to the whiteboard. Foxes, badgers, rabbits, nesting birds and so on all live in our hedgerows.

The teacher goes into role as a farmer by putting on some green wellies. He tells the children he's had a letter from the council. He reads it to the children. The letter is then passed around. It is a *truthful fake*. It looks official. It reads:

Dear Farmer Joseph,

We understand that in previous years the Council has had its annual bonfire in one of your fields. This year we need the biggest field you have because, as well as the fire itself, we are going to install a roller coaster. This is very exciting and we know you will want to continue your excellent reputation by giving us what we need.

Do get in touch if you need to.

Yours sincerely
Mrs Jackson
Leader of the Council

The original letter is left out whilst a copy is displayed on the whiteboard. The teacher (stepping out of role) goes through the letter and checks understanding – words like *previous, annual, bonfire* and *reputation*. The teacher asks:

- What have we found out about Farmer Joseph?

- What is important to Farmer Joseph?

- What's the first thing Farmer Joseph needs to do now?

The last question stimulates much discussion. Eventually it's decided that the gate needs to be widened in order to get the roller coaster in. At this point, the teacher throws in a hand grenade (not literally), back in role as Farmer Joseph, rubbing his chin:

One of those hedges needs to come down. I'm certain of that.

The teacher and the children 'map out' where the sticky notes representing the animals and birds are. One of the hedges does indeed need to come down ... And on it goes.

This is just a brief example of a pathway – around 25 minutes or so. I've left it at the point where the dilemma-grenade has been chucked in. How does it tie into the RAVE curriculum I mentioned above? Well, here's my attempt at answering that (it's a little easier for me as I was the teacher):

- **R:** It's a rural farming community. The children told me loads about their weekends spent helping their parents with chores. They also told me of the fun they have. It was also late October so Bonfire Night was looming.

- **A:** The children were required to recall previous learning around habitats that they had done with their regular teacher. They needed to select a feature from this learning (in this case an animal name and perhaps the name of its habitat) to place on a sticky note around the classroom.

- **V:** The children were hitting the PLTS as described above. In a short time, the children had worked individually and as part of a large group, contributing to discussion and *moving the story on* (more of this later).

- **E:** As well as teacher praise and continual feedback on how work was progressing, evaluation appeared in the deconstruction of the letter from the council, the checking of understanding and through careful questioning.

As well as realising these points, the lesson was a little different because:

- I was a visitor modelling classroom practice
- The tables were moved out of the way
- There were more adults than usual in the classroom

It was also different for *us kids* because:

- We were allowed to have loads of ideas
- We were able to say what we thought
- We were given sticky notes to attach up on the wall where we wanted
- We could talk about our lives at the same time as doing what that bloke was asking us to do
- All our responses seemed to be right
- In a good way we were all the same
- That bloke seemed to know a lot about us all when he'd finished

I could go on, but you have a go now. Respond (in your head or on some paper) to the following:

- What do you need to teach tomorrow?
- Get a picture of the class in your mind ...
- How can you get the content to resonate with the children?
- What can you *surprise* them with?
- What dilemmas can bubble to the surface in the topic you are covering?
- How can a mundane piece of study be RAVE-d?

 Things that don't get classes buzzing about learning

1   Miserable teachers

2   Miserable teachers who bang on

3   Miserable teachers who bang on about stuff

4   Miserable teachers who bang on about stuff that's got nothing to do with the topic

5   Miserable teachers who bang on about stuff that's got nothing to do with the topic and who pay no attention

6   Miserable teachers who bang on about stuff that's got nothing to do with the topic and who pay no attention to questions

7   Miserable teachers who bang on about stuff that's got nothing to do with the topic and who pay no attention to questions or answers

8   Miserable teachers who bang on about stuff that's got nothing to do with the topic and who pay no attention to questions or answers which actually would open up interesting learning

9   Miserable teachers who bang on about stuff that's got nothing to do with the topic and who pay no attention to questions or answers which actually would open up interesting learning journeys that could get kids buzzing

10   The sentence: 'I've got a detailed PowerPoint presentation to prepare you for your test'

Here's a picture of what I'm trying to say:

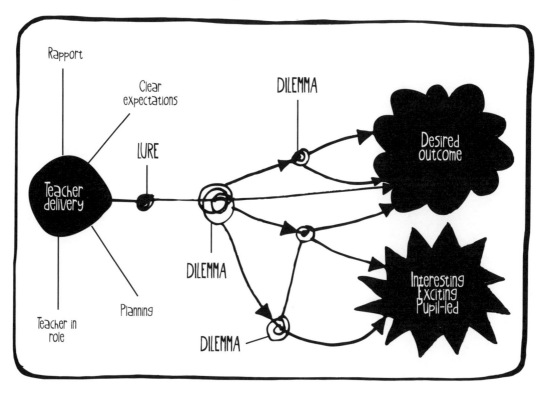

Using the RAVE idea, coupled with the concept of luring children into learning and introducing dilemmas (shifting the hedge), will hopefully give you some ideas of your own. Looking at the picture above, could you apply this thinking to your own planning?

Basically, you have a choice …

A few years ago I worked with a teacher – let's call him Mr Quint – who was facing the sack on account of his poor teaching. He was a very knowledgeable man and knew the ins and outs of the profession. He acted as if he didn't really like kids and you were often left wondering how the heck he managed to get himself out of bed every morning. Anyway, I was asked to support Mr Quint as he was on his very last chance in terms of pulling a satisfactory lesson out of the bag. Mr Quint wouldn't meet me at lunchtime or after school so he got one of his classes covered (strangely defeating the object, I felt) and I used a non-contact lesson.

I asked Mr Quint to bring along a 45-minute lesson plan for his next class of 12-year-olds – the one where he was going to be observed by Mr Hooper (head of department) and Chief Brody (head teacher). Mr Quint presented me with a very mundane lesson around a theme and showed me a copy of the worksheet the children would fill in as a result of their 'learning'. It was only good in the sense that it offered us a starting point.

Mr Quint was a specialist in Maths but it appeared that he had stopped trying quite a long time before we found ourselves sitting together. This is a model of what he gave me – the shape of his proposed lesson:

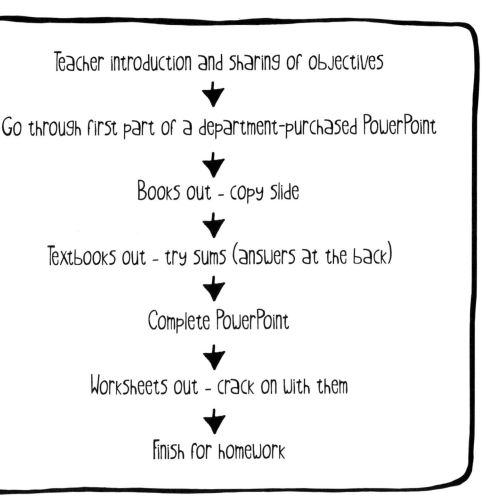

Now, to be fair, Mr Quint had ticked the following:

☑ Use of ICT

☑ Building on prior learning

☑ Objectives shared

☑ Homework set

There may have been other things but, on the evidence before me, Maths was well boring. And Mr Quint was heading for the door. So, using all the Maths-Drama-sense I could muster, I co-planned a buzzing Maths lesson. I hadn't really got the RAVE model in my head at that time, but I knew that the mathematical messages Mr Quint was trying to communicate needed overhauling and selling to the children. Otherwise, they were going to take him to the cleaners. Like they regularly did.

Mr Quint was very open to my suggestions and we sketched out an alternative lesson that would fulfil the same objectives (and a little more). As a picture, it looked a bit like this:

Teacher introduction and objectives shared

↓

A key question shared around the potential real-life application
of the Maths skill to be learned

↓

Brainstorming in groups on big paper

↓

Brainstorms stuck up on wall

↓

One pupil stays with the brainstorm while the rest of the group visit
other displays - bit like an art gallery

↓

Teacher-led explanation on whiteboard of new skill

↓

Paired work applying the skill

↓

Teacher introduces scenarios where the new skill can be applied: How many tiles
do we need to pave the floor of the new kitchen? How many logs will we need
to roll the stone cubes to the pyramid site?

↓

Children in groups of three or four working through the challenges whilst
Mr Quint moves around the room spotlighting groups applying the skill

↓

The lesson plenary is pupils explaining the skill to the rest of the class
using their own scenarios

↓

Homework set builds on the plenary and is to consider and list other applications
of this mathematical skill, to be shared at the start of the next lesson

Mr Quint and I agreed that this was the lesson that was going to pleasantly surprise Mr Hooper and Chief Brody. He was going to catch them out with this one, and no mistake. In our new version of the original lesson we could tick off the following features of a reasonable (satisfactory) lesson, which is all that Hooper and Brody wanted to see:

☑ Use of ICT

☑ Effective starter

☑ Connections to previous learning

☑ Objectives shared

☑ Developing resilience

☑ Varying groupings

☑ Spotlighting good progress

☑ Homework set

You could add:

☑ **Relevance** steeped in the brainstorm starter activity

☑ **Academic** in the potential application of the new skill

☑ **Vocational** in the starter, the group work and the plenary

☑ **Evaluation** is present during the gallery, in the group work and in the plenary

---

Invigorated teaching brings these four objectives together. All good stuff then.

I saw Mr Quint after his observation. I was really interested to see how he'd got on with our super plan. I was particularly curious because I'm hopeless at Maths and was particularly excited about having helped him plan a Maths lesson.

'How did it go?' I asked enthusiastically. 'Oh, I didn't do it. I just did the original. Your stuff isn't for me,' came the nonchalant reply. And he walked off – *like his job didn't depend on it!*

I was gobsmacked. He'd made his choice. I couldn't believe it. I'm not saying the lesson was a model Maths lesson or that it was breaking new barriers *but* it was a damn sight better than the one he delivered. What the hell were Hooper and the Brody going to think? They'd watched him teach it. They must've wondered what the heck I was doing, never mind Mr Quint!

Mr Quint left the school on an early retirement deal struck up with the local authority. He'd destroyed Maths for many children over the years because he'd made the wrong choice. He could've turned it round, gone for it and shown the powers that be that he did have the capacity to change. Unfortunately, he didn't. It was his call, and he blew it. Through the lens of the model in Chapter 2, he was a Big Old Sleepy Bear who had drifted into the quadrant of the The Ungrateful Dead. And he'd just allowed himself to be shot straight through the head. Bang!

Here are some thoughts. Don't worry, these keep me awake at night as well!

You own what goes on in your classroom

You are in charge of the curriculum

If it is engaging, it is because you have made it so

If it's boring, you are boring – sort it out!

Finally for this chapter ...

 Things your curriculum needs in your classroom

1   Clear expectations

2   Happiness

3   Measured and reasonable responses

4   Thinking time

5   Dilemmas and problems that need sorting out

6   Ownership over what you are teaching and what the children are learning

7 Rapport

8 RAVE

9 A hole that you've dug and then covered in leaves

10 Children

(Don't be a Quint.) Right, read on ...

- STEP 1: Dig hole

- STEP 2: Cover with branches

OR Holes and Branches ...

OR Finding the Curriculum Whilst Meeting the Needs of the National Curriculum (which, remember is only a suggested curriculum)

Accidentally Learning

There is no need to be joined together at the head, as long as we are joined together at the heart.

Margaret Wheatley

The earth without 'art' is just 'eh?'

Seen on Twitter

 Things to stop children in their tracks:

1   **You start singing Puccini's aria *Nessun dorma*:** Why start singing an aria? Because, after the initial shock, the lads in the PE lesson I was covering all started joining in. Showing my age a bit with this one, but *Nessun dorma* was part of a cultural hangover from Italia '90, along with Gazza's tears, and was still being sung on terraces years later. Belting out this beauty enabled me to get on with the lesson rather than getting taken to the cleaners as I suspected I was about to be.

2   **You juggle cats:** I don't mean juggle actual cats. That would be cruel and potentially dangerous. The great comedian and banjo player Steve Martin would use cat juggling as part of his stand-up routine in the 1970s. The bizarreness of the act would be enough to have audiences in hysterics and utterly gripped by what might be coming next. That's essentially what we want in our classes, isn't it? Well, maybe not the hysterics, but we want the gripped-ness, the sudden tension that will lead to positive learning tension. When I did this most recently, the cats were left stranded high up in three different areas of the classroom and needed rescuing. The class of 5-year-olds I was working

with were just the people to mount the rescue and invented an array of weird and wonderful contraptions in order to get the cats down safely. Buzzing.

3   **You are a wiz with a Diablo:** A Diabolo is a Chinese yo-yo and my colleague was ruddy great at using it. He could've been on *Blue Peter*. If the kids were good, had finished their work and were successful in meeting the lesson objectives, he'd whiz out the Diabolo and chuck it around for a bit. They loved it.

4   **The classroom has been rearranged so the desks and chairs face the back:** Children can be flummoxed by a change in the usual.

5   **Change your hairstyle:** Children can be flummoxed by a change in the usual and can be visibly shaken by a teacher's attempt at an aggressive comb-over.

6   **Turn the classroom into a *CSI*-style crime scene:** You can't beat a gaffa-tape outline of a body in the middle of your floor. It might not necessarily be the outline of a human ...

7   **Be seated at the front with a dog:** Every so often, the drudge of day-to-day school life is powerfully awakened by the arrival in school of the Littlest Hobo; stray dogs should always be approached with caution but are a great way of altering the moods of children. More dogs in school I say!

Seriously (kind of), we had this situation where a dog ended up with me in my classroom as I was awaiting the arrival of my class. It belonged to a boy in my form who was en route to collect it. When the class came in they were of course completely surprised by the vision of One Man and his Dog at the front of the classroom. I told the children he was a witness to a miscarriage of justice and that they needed to interview him (the dog that is, not the man).

8   **Speak a different language:** What languages do dogs speak? Well you can figure it out for yourself, can't you? If a dog barks loudly, what is she saying?

Stop!
No!
Be careful!
There are a number of children trapped in the collapsed mine ...

Or if the dog whimpers, is she saying:

Sorry.
Why?
I liked him but it's over now.

If she snarls and bares her fangs, is she saying?

That's the last time you hit me.
I'm warning you.
I've seen stuff I need to tell you about and you're not listening to me.

You can basically create a vocabulary for a dog made up of sounds that children can then translate. I saw this done by Warwick University Drama Professor Joe Winston and it worked a treat. It inspired me to go out and buy a puppet dog which I was determined to shoehorn into my teaching somehow. It worked and here she is:

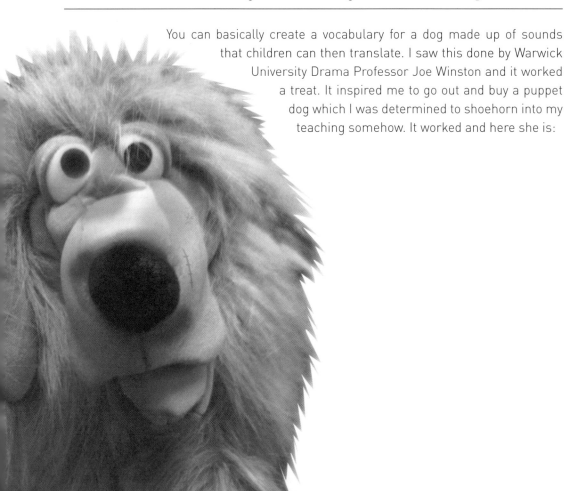

It's a prop that stops kids in their tracks when they see me with it. Then we start hot seating it and she responds with vocabulary for us all to decipher. This isn't always the best route with Key Stage 4 Science, but the younger end are often thrilled, want to stroke her and ask her questions about her dog's life. As teacher–puppeteer, I'm secretly in charge of the action. Bit like teaching really.

Just a quick word about hot seating: This is a popular Drama convention where children ask a character (often a teacher in role) key questions. The danger with this technique is that the children are not always given enough time to prepare good questions that will challenge and inform. So what often happens is that Florence Nightingale is asked who her favourite football team is, if she likes Lady Gaga and who she fancies at the moment. Highlighting the importance of questions for hot seating can be prepared like this:

- Introduce the idea that Florence Nightingale will be arriving in ten minutes

- On scrap paper the children brainstorm questions they'd like to ask Flo

- Ask them to reject any questions that ask about the kinds of things I've mentioned above, plus any that touch on McDonald's, David Cameron, Google, Facebook and so on

- Get the children to list three really good questions – you could pair them up to do this

- Give out sticky notes and ask the children to pick their best question from the three and write them on a note

- When Flo 'arrives', the questions on the sticky notes are asked. If there's repetition, one of the other top three questions could be posed instead

- A question can only be asked if the child is holding the 'microphone'. The microphone could be a marker pen, a rubber chicken, a scarf, a ruler … anything. Basically, if you aren't holding the mic, you can't speak. Try it, it works!

- At the end of the Q&A, Flo 'leaves'. Collect up the sticky notes and display them. You can then move into a news report based on the answers. The questions on the sticky notes essentially jog the children's memories as they prepare their work

Anyway, back to surprises. Speaking in a different language can thrill some children especially if it's the language of the lesser known Niarb tribe from the distant planet Llabeye. Or you could just speak Welsh.

9   **Grab a piano and sing 'I Don't Like Mondays' by the Boomtown Rats:** And by this I don't mean you have to go and learn the piano. Just demonstrate a skill you have as a way of engaging children immediately into the space. As it happens, as a result of my misspent college years, I can play this ditty on the piano. From this came a serious and rigorous piece of Drama study around American high school gun massacres. We also used the visual texts (i.e. films) *Bowling for Columbine* (2002, Michael Moore) and *Elephant* (2003, Gus Van Sant) to support our learning – the former a documentary, the latter a docu-drama. From these stimuli (music and film) we created live Drama. The piano had been moved into my room for some singing rehearsals that were taking place over the following weekend. And, never one to miss a trick, I was happy for the interruption.

10   **Build something *really* big. I mean *really really* big:** When do we ever let children build something really big? Something that will fill the hall, never mind the classroom? Big like a spaceship? This might sound great for the little ones, but I saw this happen profoundly with a large group of 13-year-old pupils in a school that was being closed. There's a book that needs to be written about these children one day, however, all I'll say here is that they had been going through an experience of school that was basically knackered. All the children had known was special measures and something had to give. I went into the school with a brilliant group of educational artists (www. thriftmusictheatre.co.uk) with the remit to work with the staff and the children to offer a curriculum that would be engaging and offer new experiences to the pupils, as well as invigorating the practice of the teachers. The first thing we did was build a very big spaceship out of junk. It gave the teachers a term's work and the 13-year-olds loved it.

A spaceship

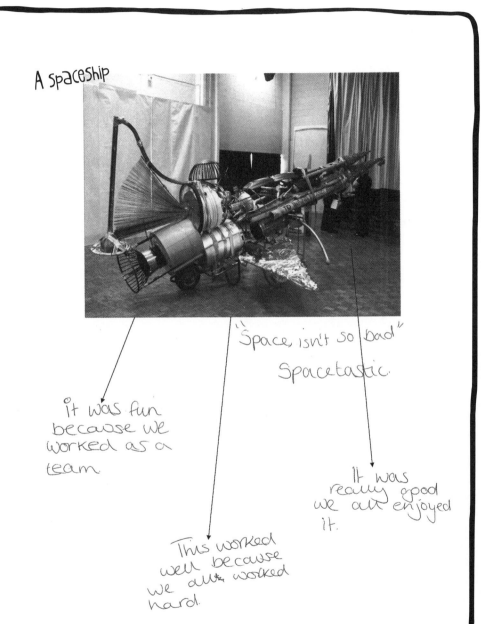

"Space isn't so bad"

Spacetastic.

It was fun because we worked as a team.

This worked well because we all worked hard.

It was really good we all enjoyed it.

As you can see, these are just some of my examples (except number 3). Number 10 is an extreme example of stopping kids in their tracks as it relied on practitioners visiting the school. Having said that, it was just for a day and yet it acted as springboard for a sustained piece of work.

None of these examples had learning objectives attached to them, none of them started life in a scheme of work and all of them were the results of *planned accidents*. These are the types of situations that often we need to gear up for and are central to the whole idea of hooking kids into learning. Some people might call it 'having a bit about yer'.

Once upon a time

It's hard to think back now but once upon a time we had no technology in the classroom. No interactive whiteboards, no Internet access and no cameras. We had tables, chairs, books and some paper. If we were lucky (or organised), we had a tub with glue sticks, felt tips and scissors. I was working with a school recently that was about to move into a new state-of-the-art building (a beautiful product of the now-defunct Building Schools for the Future programme). This was a secondary school in a historically tough area and the new build was going to offer a fresh start for many – teachers and pupils alike. A fortnight before the real physical move, all IT resources, hardware and software were removed from the decrepit old building. Classrooms were suddenly bereft of interactive whiteboards and the like – essentially, as if by magic, the classrooms had defaulted to how they would have looked fifteen or twenty years ago. Back to basics, in other words.

What was really interesting in this very unscientific scenario were the reactions of the people in the building. The classroom-bound teachers who had been brought up on a diet of technology were really challenged when it was taken away. Teachers of Physical Education and the Arts fared better – the technology in these areas has always been simple; if the space was there it could be filled with meaningful activity. It was rather sweet that experienced teachers who had been in the profession for many years got kind of misty-eyed, as if an old world order had been restored and that things could be just how they used to be.

Bottom line: If you've nothing in the classroom but yourself, you need to get yourself buzzing by being brave, brainy and bothered.

Some of the teachers during this *Twilight Zone*-like fortnight, bereft of technological support, actually had the time of their lives. The established norms were out of the window and suddenly individual teachers, as scary as it seemed, were taking hold of the curriculum in their own spaces and running down that metaphorical woodland path that hardly anyone else walks down …

I'm not trying to suggest that technology stifles creative and innovative approaches; I'm merely stating that when we're without it, we teachers sometimes have to work better, and when we work better, surprising things can happen.

 Things getting skipped in a moving school

1 Knackered old spider plants

2 Exam syllabi from the mid-1990s

3 National Strategies folders

4 Minutes of forgotten meetings

5 Audio cassettes

6 VHS copies of *Blackadder*

7 Textbooks

8 Banda-copied worksheets

9 Overhead projectors

10 Memories of children gone

I was working back at the new state-of-the-art school recently – with its shopping centre style facades and walkways, its huge panes of glass and its light, lots of lovely light – and it was brilliant. I stopped a child of the hooded variety and asked him what he thought of the new school. 'Same shit, different building,' he replied. You can't please everyone all the time, but you can try your damnedest!

Web 1.0

I've mentioned elsewhere my love of pen and paper as technology for learning – Web 1.0 if you like. Here's a piece of work I do a lot with children and young people of all ages. I discovered it by accident when I was sharing some other work with teachers on Mantle of the Expert.

In that piece, we were looking at fictional contexts that could be built around the study of mountain ranges in Geography, so we drew a mountain range. Unfortunately, I only had A3 paper rather than the roll of lining paper I would normally use. So each teacher took their sheet of paper and used a fat pen to horizontally divide it in two with an imaginary mountain range, like this:

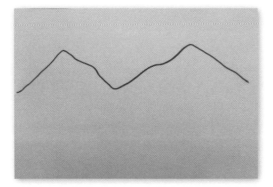

When the teachers brought their drawings to the centre of the space, I realised there was an alternative to the mountain range work I was planning to do. So I did this:

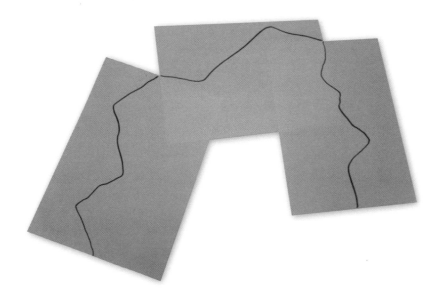

Suddenly the outline of an island was emerging.

 Things to do when learning accidents happen

1 Tolerate uncertainty

2 Vocalise the accident to the people with you

3 Remain calm and positive

4 Go with the flow – the accident might make your lesson more exciting

5 Immediately mine the possibilities

6 Distribute the thinking; don't keep your questions to yourself

7 Reflect on your learning objectives but don't let them act as blockers to potentially new and exciting diversions

8 Be realistic in the potential of the new direction. For example, if you have been happily working with the children on arranging a bonfire party for the local community, then to have the world invaded by super-aliens might not be totally appropriate

9 See the opportunity rather than fear the chaos

10 Let these learning accidents act as *turning points* in the learning story you are telling. Mantle of the Expert guru Luke Abbott calls these 'crux moments'. Essentially they are the traps of learning that we've unwittingly fallen into ourselves. Nice one!

 Great celluloid crux moments or turning points

1 The huge shark making its first real appearance to Chief Martin Brody in *Jaws*, prompting the line 'We're gonna need a bigger boat'

2 Darth Vader revealing himself as Luke Skywalker's father in *The Empire Strikes Back*

3 Cinderella leaving her shoe behind

4 The Scarecrow speaking to Dorothy in *The Wizard Of Oz*

5 The Snowman magically coming to life

6 Bruno becoming the Boy in the Striped Pyjamas as he sneaks under the fence into Auschwitz

7 Chitty Chitty Bang Bang taking to the air

8 Marion Crane getting sliced and diced in Norman Bates' shower in the middle of *Psycho* (after audiences thought that the film was about her and had invested their emotions in her)

9 Lucy entering the wardrobe in *The Lion, the Witch and the Wardrobe*

10 Billy frittering away his brother's betting money in *Kes*

So where are these turning points in our own teaching? What stories are we telling? How are the children gripped by a twist or a dilemma?

Think of a piece of learning you are planning. Where are the turning points? Where are the uncertainties? Where does the potential for learning accidents exist?

I'll carry on with my 'island accident' in a moment, but first ... an example of a great learning accident.

Using the idea of the children creating a BIG picture, a teacher I worked with recently asked a child to draw a tree into the landscape that was being created. Now, in the teacher's mind, the child was going to draw something akin to a fir tree. This is what the child drew:

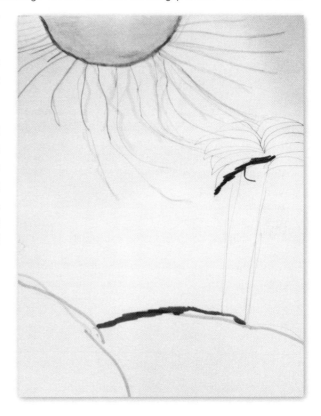

It's a palm tree under a blazing sun. The opposite of what the teacher had anticipated. Suddenly the whole context of learning was shifting whilst the teacher watched the palm tree materialise.

Next, the teacher asked his 7-year-olds to add some features to the hills surrounding the trees. He expected the children to add walls and more forests, but now the children had shifted the *climate* of the context to that of a warm place. Unpredictably, the children drew some caves and tunnels on the sides of the hills:

A child then added a figure near one of these tunnels which allowed the following questions to emerge:

- Who is the person near the tunnel?
- Why do they look worried?
- Have they been in the tunnel?
- Have they got a secret?
- Have they told their Mummy?
- Does he need our help?

- What's inside the tunnel?

- How deep is the tunnel?

- Can we go in the tunnel?

This was taking the teacher in all sorts of unpredictable directions. And whilst the curriculum was bubbling to the surface via these happy learning accidents, the teacher was also deciding what text the class were going to study next: *The Tunnel* by Anthony Browne. Sorted.

Having the capacity to make these snap decisions may appear to be the workings of a skilled maverick, but as you can see from this anecdote, the (indeed skilled) teacher was making professional judgements and decisions in response to the *human* reactions of the children. This is indeed

BRAVE.

Here's something we can add to the curriculum model we talked about earlier:

Relevant

Academic

Vocational

Evaluation

Let's add the word *buzzing* (as in, engaging and exciting) to make our brand spanking new BRAVE curriculum:

Buzzing

Relevant

Academic

Vocational

Evaluation

The teacher in this situation was all of these, and processing it all in *real time*. This isn't maverick-madness; it's responding to the children in front of you and reacting to their view of the world. Being the school's numeracy co-ordinator, the teacher also needed to add in the following learning around mathematics to the big picture:

• Simple fractions

• Length and area

• Analogue and digital time-telling

• Volume

• Collecting data

Is it really such a big leap to take the learning around these concepts and place them in a context? In this case, a community in a warm climate with a dragon problem. Yes, a problem with a dragon. And a pyramid that needs building. And all sorts of other things that were emerging.

Where's the Maths? Well, let's take the pyramid issue: where does the mathematics curriculum lie in the design and construction of a pyramid? I'll leave that one with you.

Back to my island ...

So there I am, working with teachers, doing mountains, but suddenly I'm faced with an island emerging in front of me on the table. Fantastic. An opportunity! An accident! So an internal monologue kicks in ...

Okay, it's not a mountain range at all. It's an island. I'll still do what I was going to do but the direction will change. An island. A desolate island. An island community. Not like that TV show *Lost* with the hopeless ending. This island doesn't have an ending. It's in the *now*.

People have got to live here so that I can hang the tension on something. Maybe there's just one person.

An old lady? She doesn't want to move. I won't tell them about her yet.

Why is she on her own? Why has she been left behind? How does she live?

St Kilda.

St Kilda?

The remote island community off the coast of Scotland that died when people decided to return to the mainland.

Yes, a community that abandoned itself. Got into boats and rowed away.

Leaving the island in a state of *Mary Celeste*-ness.

Except for the old woman ... living on her own.

Is she magic?

The teachers gathered around as my thoughts raced, as the accident morphed into a direction, an opportunity. The papers joined together and the teachers enjoyed the surprise of seeing the outline of the island form in front of them.

'Right, I need you to add some detail on your drawing for me.' I asked the teachers to add the following to their own sheets, giving them time between each request:

- Landscape features – beaches, hills, caves, etc. (Where is the Geography here?)

- Agree with each other the *scale* of the drawing. In other words, how big everything is. What is the size of the beach? How far is the mainland? We agree this and write it elsewhere (when I do this with children, it goes on a fact sheet or on the whiteboard equivalent)

- I then asked the teachers to mark the *human* features of the island. Before the fat pens hit the paper though, there's this caveat:

This is an island that has been left behind many years ago. It was deserted perhaps post-war; there is no evidence of urbanisation, but there is evidence of old industry.

(With children, I'll say: There is no evidence of shops, cars, fast-food drive-thrus, sports shops, modern technology. This is a step back in time.)

Typical human features that appear in this exercise

1   A pier

2   Back-to-back cottages

3   A school

4   A lighthouse

5   A pub

More interesting human features that can also appear in this exercise

1   A castle

2   A mined beach

3   A prison

4   A coastal path

5   A shipwreck

6   A graveyard

7   A tin mine

8   Underground storm shelters

9   A palace

10 A zoo

Interesting natural features I've seen emerge in this task

1 A natural well

2 A puffin colony

3 A volcano

4 Quicksand

5 A dark forest

I particularly like the idea of the *dark forest* which conjures up all sorts of possibilities for learning directions (and accidents!). Children (especially boys) are gripped by this particular feature, so if you try this idea, get a dark forest banged onto the island somewhere. I think it goes back to the fairy tales we all were told as little children. There's always a dark forest. Even in modern storytelling, the dark forest looms large. Look at *Harry Potter*. Then ask yourself: where does the curriculum lie in a dark forest? This question is essentially the *key* question when building contexts, and you'll see it used a lot in this book. If you hadn't guessed, it's a mantra to me!

When introducing this island context to teachers, we populate the outline with features. We then unpick the curriculum question. Because of my background, I naturally lean towards the Arts and Humanities. It's due to this that I try really hard to focus on Science, Mathematics and Technology (with a bit of MFL (Modern Foreign Languages) thrown in for good measure).

Taking the example of the dark forest, can you see the Science curriculum potential for our younger children that could emerge from this particular context? What about:

• Growing plants

• Light

• Living things

• Plants and animals

• Habitats

Staying with the dark forest, what about the key concepts in the Maths curriculum we offer our older kids:

- Competence
- Creativity
- Applications and implications
- Critical understanding

How can we use the island context to uncover this learning? Perhaps we could *extend the fiction* in order to broaden the Maths work?

What if ... the island has been purchased by a company responsible for some of the greatest theme parks in the world? Where is the Maths in this (bear in mind I'm a Drama teacher)?

- Measurement
- Weather forecasting
- Calculating insurance
- Collecting and processing data
- Probability

There are hopefully stacks more. Leaving Maths alone for a moment, the questions that emerge for me when offered this scenario are:

- Which buildings should be preserved?
- Is it right that a private company can buy an island?
- What happens to the puffins?
- Can the prison be turned into a hotel?
- How will tourists get to the island?
- What is the weather like on the island? Will it be good for business?

Let's ratchet it up a gear and start thinking about *points of view*.

The Company
We're the biggest theme park company in the world. What questions emerge when taking this point of view?

- How much is this going to cost?

- Will people be concerned about the environmental impact of our purchase?

- How do we ensure our workers are safe on the island?

- Who do we talk to in order to find out more about the place?

- Which bits do we try to preserve?

- What could be the subject of our theme park?

- What natural features of the island could we turn into selling points?

- How can we keep everyone happy?

- Do we have to keep everyone happy?

- Who do we need to keep happy?

The Government

- Is the island ours to sell?

- When did the island become ours to sell?

- Are we certain it's depopulated?

- How can we preserve history whilst allowing redevelopment?

- Should the island be left alone?

- How many jobs could the development of a theme park bring?

- How many other mainland businesses will benefit?

- What will the environmental impact be of development?

- What if the theme park fails? Who will pick up the pieces?

- Would it be more profitable for the Government to lease the island rather than sell it?

The Environmentalist

- What about the puffins to the east of the island?

- What will be the impact of building of a ferry terminal on the ocean and the land?

- How will the island be powered?

- How and where will waste be disposed?

- How are the Government going to manage the actions of the Company?

- Will independent groups be allowed to monitor the building work and eventual running of the park?

- Will sites of historical interest and natural beauty still be free to visit?

- Do we have to have a roller coaster?

- Will food and drink come from local mainland sources?

- Will the development be a theme park that happens to be on an island, or will it be an island that also happens to have a theme park?

When I was working with the teachers and the concept of the island emerged, followed by the theme park idea, I realised we needed a twist, a *crux moment*. I decided that this should emerge in the form of a person. In a way, after the human and physical elements of the island (the Geography, the History) have been established, bringing in these points of view is the natural next step. I hope you can see that this goes far and beyond personal and social education, but it is always good to bring it right back to a simple dilemma.

This is the dilemma I offered the teachers I was working with, and one which I have used with lots of classes since:

The purchase of the island is going through smoothly with Government, Company and Environmentalists all in agreement with the way forward. Then something unpredictable happens. A message is received stating that someone is still living on the island. Someone who has never left. Someone the community left behind when it deserted its shores in the 1950s. An old woman now, she lives in the seemingly empty lighthouse.

This generates sudden questions, of course, be it from teachers or children:

- How did we not know about her?
- How does she live?
- Why did she choose to stay?
- Where are her family?
- Who loves her?
- Did she ever marry?
- How can she be happy so alone?
- How does she cope without utilities?
- Is she not scared?
- What does her typical day look like?
- Can she stay on the island with the development work?
- Who should decide her fate?
- Is she a block to the progress of the project?
- Should she be protected, like the puffins?
- To whom does she speak?
- Does she speak English?
- Is she in good health?
- Is she educated?
- Has she ever been to the mainland?

There is the opportunity here to prepare a class for a really interesting hot-seating activity – with time, of course, given to the generation of really ace questions. Before this, however there are other fascinating opportunities such as:

- A meeting between the Government and the Company to decide on the best way forward

- The Company considering how the old woman could actually fit into the plans for the theme park

- Social services working out how to support the old woman

- A press conference

All these things can be done in your classroom. Remember the *points of view* of the parties involved.

This is where I often take the work having introduced the idea of the old woman:

We need to go and see her. Who should go? What are we going to say?

This takes some planning and can take the form of group work, with individuals in each team adopting the different points of view. For example, a group of four-plus youngsters could have in it representatives of:

- The Company

- The Government

- Social services

And letting your imagination go a little:

- A descendent of those who left the community

- A speech therapist

- An appropriate adult (an independent person who ensures the old woman is protected)

- The police

I hope you'll see a variety of possibilities here and, wrapped within it, opportunities for discussion, time for reflection and new ideas surfacing. Obviously the roles that emerge may depend on the age of the children with whom you are working. In expanding the fiction I am not turning my back on the learning objectives I may have for my class. For example, in the journey I have described so far, I could be hitting these learning objectives:

- To produce a piece of formal writing from a certain point of view

- To work in a group to solve a human dilemma

- To use Drama to develop empathy

These are just examples and it all depends on *who* and *what* you are teaching and what the learning intentions are.

When I first tried this with a primary school class, the group, working in role as grown-ups preparing to go and see the old woman, attempted to script the conversations that might happen on meeting the old lady. This threw up its own set of dilemmas such as: How can we predict what she will say? and What if she doesn't speak our language? The children asked me what they should do and I simply responded: 'Be as prepared as you can.'

This got them thinking about what they would need in order for a successful trip to take place. This might be a good way to go with younger children – a *bag-packing* exercise.

 Great bags to pack with your class

1 A trip to the moon

2 A voyage to the North Pole

3 A climb up the Eiger

4 A journey to the Magical Land of Oz

5 A tour of the Middle East

6 A trip to Uganda

7 A time-travel trip to 1066

8 A sojourn to the Somme

9 A sail up the Nile

10 A problem-solving trip to an until-recently-thought-uninhabited island …

Healthy learning tension

In the story ...

So, we get to the island. It's a clear day and the landing is safe. We go in the direction of the lighthouse. The message we received about the woman on the island didn't tell us anything about her. Not even her name. We approach the towering lighthouse and approach the door ...

Meanwhile, in the classroom ... the children stand in front of a 'door' – the door to the lighthouse. We rehearse who is going to say what. I tell them that I will provide the voice of the old woman. *Always* when I simply state the fact that I will be *representing* a character, the children *believe* it instantly. I offer to do it to keep the story alive and it always works.

There is generally a good discussion about who should knock on the door. If it doesn't happen, simply ask, 'Who is going to knock?' That leads to a shifting of eyes and uncertainty (= great learning tension).

This is what happened most recently when I did this with a class. I provided the voice of the old lady and eventually emerged from the gloom. I didn't have a silly voice or an outfit. I didn't have my hair in curlers and I wasn't smoking a cigarette. It was just me representing someone else and engaging some kids in their learning. Not at all *Dramarama*.

By accident, it emerged that the old woman had a lot of questions for the visitors. Pausing the action, I told the children to prepare for a meeting with the old lady where she would be asking them questions of her own. This required the children to return to their groups and begin *predicting* what the old woman might want to know. They of course began generating questions of their own.

This is what the old woman asked:

- How did you get here?
- Why are you so smart?
- What's with all the paperwork?
- What is it you want?
- Who sent you?

The children, in their roles, answered as best they could and I just listened. Remember the list of things that can stop children in their tracks (such as cat juggling) at the beginning of this chapter? Those crazy skills pale into insignificance beside the cool response of a character who is living and breathing inside a context in which we are all working. Check this out for an exchange between me (as the woman) and a child (as a theme park rep):

Child:	We've come to see if you'd be happy to move away.
Woman:	I don't need to.
Child:	We need you to.
Woman:	Really? I don't want to.
Child:	I understand. It's just that we're buying the island and you can't live here anymore.

I-should-have-gone-to-RADA-type pause.

Woman:	I see. Well. That's impossible.
Child:	Why?

Wait for it …

Woman:	It's impossible, because I *own* the island.

Now that really did stop the children in their tracks! This was unscripted, real and seat-of-yer-pants stuff. For the children it was gob-smacking. The old woman owned the island! The implications were huge! Who was selling it then? Where was the evidence? And so on.

This was a lovely learning accident that had popped into my head, and I know where the idea had come from. On a wall in our house I have an original framed cinema poster for the wonderful film *Local Hero* from 1983. If you've not seen it, you should. If you have seen it, you'll remember that a huge Texan oil company is attempting to buy out a coastal town in the North of Scotland. It then turns out that (*SPOILER ALERT*) much of the land is owned by beachcomber Fulton Mackay who lives in a shack made from upturned boats. This came to mind as the child was talking to me, and then suddenly the fiction spun in a new direction. This is a happy accident, a great turning point and a memorable crux moment!

It also offered a rich direction for the children to take the work in. The solving of a fresh dilemma: the Company is buying an island from an organisation which doesn't actually own it.

Other things that popped into my head when being the old woman:

- I wonder if they've seen the night beast yet
- The lighthouse will collapse during the next violent storm
- I hope the dead don't rise again tonight
- They're in for a shock when they discover they are trapped here forever
- The dark forest will have them. And their bones
- I'm going to poison the tea
- A trip away would be nice
- None of them have stepped into my bear traps yet
- These people might make the voices stop
- My name is Melody Strange

Of course, I only shared the last one with the children. And so it went on. Problems to be solved, dilemmas to be addressed and questions to be answered.

More recently, I did a similar island lure with another group, again in primary (8- and 9-year-olds) and this is a brief summary of how it played out, accidents and everything:

A coastal protest

1 What do we know about the sea?
2 Create the island as described earlier (separate sheets of paper linked together by a coastline)
3 The sea is swallowing the island – what options does the *community* have?
4 A *team* is called in to help advise on the sea defences that should be put into place

5   The *owner* of the island does not want their help because he feels the defences will ruin the landscape

6   The *community* protest

This is what the learning journey looked like in the classroom:

- A Q&A session along the lines of:
  - » Does anyone know anything about the sea?
  - » Have we ever been to an island?
  - » Can we drink seawater?

- Make coastline and notice the features that have been created. By *notice*, I mean that the teacher (in this case, me) highlights ideas that the children have placed on the paper. It may sound strange but when noticing, you *make it explicit*:

I notice Ben and Samir have drawn a house. I wonder what living in the house is like? I notice that it's near the sea. Is that where the people who live in the house get their drinking water from?

I notice Charlotte and Olivia have drawn a castle. I notice that it looks very big. I wonder if anyone lives there? And I wonder who built it?

- Having noticed elements of all the pictures (and therefore investing *all* the children in the context), the teacher *protects* the children into the story by asking them about the people on the island. Baggage can be left at the door and the teacher can use strategies and techniques to bring the children to the edges of their seats. More of this later. The teacher talks about what life is like and then moves from talking to asking. It might sound something like this:

Teacher:	Life is tough on the island. The winters are cold and harsh. We live on the land. We live on the sea. Our food comes from the sea. What food would we have from the sea?
Child:	Fish.
Teacher:	Tell me about your fishing boat.
Child:	I have lots of Lego on my boat. And books. And a really big fishing rod.
Teacher:	We all have boats, don't we? We love the sea. Even though we love the sea, do you think we're ever scared of it?

A discussion ensues.

Teacher:	We should be perhaps. Apparently the sea will one day swallow our island. What can we do about that?
Child:	Build walls.
Teacher:	Do you think we can do that ourselves?

And so on.

We grab sticky notes and offer ideas as to how we can stop the island from being swallowed up! We *gallery* these ideas (stick them up on the wall and look at them all). Ideas include:

- Walls

- A channel through the island

- A special pipe that sucks water to the mainland

We vote on which is the best idea. When I did this with a particular group of 9-year-olds they wanted to build big walls to protect the island, almost like battlements – they had done castles the previous term! So then, we're into designing the walls thinking about materials, measurement and manpower! (Where is the numeracy in this curriculum?)

- (*LEARNING ACCIDENT ALERT*) In the particular learning journey I've described a child asked me to whom the island belonged. This little girl really caught me out (as children often do) with this question. Up until this point I had assumed that our island did indeed belong to us, the community (I hope you're noticing the shared-ness of the language: I'm in it with them – the island is *ours*). It had, up until the question, belonged to *us*.

My thought process when challenged with this question went like this:

Cripes. That's a good one. Right. Okay. Maybe we *don't* own the island. We just live there. With the landowner, who lives in the big house Thomas and Archie have drawn. This will bring tension. This will be a turning point. A dilemma. A crux moment because ... Mr Lemington Sprake owns the island. It's been in his family for years. He's a very officious man who keeps himself to himself.

- We build up a picture of Mr Sprake to the point where I can step into the role.

- The community get ready to meet Mr Sprake having prepared really ace questions to ask him. This leads to a teacher-in-role (remember, no need for funny voices or embarrassing costumes) and hot-seating session.

- The dilemma is revealed through the hot seating: Mr Sprake absolutely does not believe in big walls to protect the island.

- The community mounts a protest. We decide to picket his house having looked at some protest pictures on the Internet. We make placards and prepare to face him. Whilst the posters are being made, some children are creating chants that sum up the feeling of the community along the lines of:

We want walls!
That's what we think!
We want walls!
Or else we'll sink!

I'll jump out of my narrative here!

Hey! Secondary school teachers!

Hang on, I'm a secondary teacher by trade. If *you* are a secondary teacher, you may be wondering how these techniques might work for you. The key thing is this: these aren't just tips and techniques that I'm sharing with you. It's actually a way of thinking and delivering; it's a refining of your practice and an opportunity to reflect on how you deliver *content* to the children in your class. If you look back on the risky learning journey I've been offering to the children here, I want you to see how you could take it and use it in a secondary context. Sometimes it just comes down to *what* we need the children to learn and *how* we deliver that need.

Here's another way of putting it: translate, adapt and process the ideas here into your own classroom in the same way you would try out anything that is new to you. For example, when I first started spending more time in primary classrooms, I was fascinated by the way good teachers would talk to their children using explicit instructions like:

Sit up and look at me. Oh, Sally, that's lovely sitting. Joe, look at Sally. Isn't she sitting well. Good Joe, I can see you listening now. Well done.

There is no way you can talk to hardened secondary children in this way. But you can take away the principle and adapt it for senior students so that the above quote becomes the following:

Come on. Look at me. Thanks. Sally – cheers. Joe. Look at me. I like it when you're all looking at me! Means we can get cracking.

When settling children, it's just language. When creating stories it's just … er … language. No matter the age of the children in your class, the principles are the same. We're all in the same boat trying to engage children in their learning.

To continue, can you identify where the curriculum lies in what I've shared so far in this island story? With my senior school hat on I can see:

- **Geography:** features of the island, the water cycle

- **History:** we can spend time creating the history of the island (see Chapter 5)

- **Music:** let's write protest songs!

- **English:** let's write letters to the government asking for help with the Mr Sprake situation

- **Science:** how to make seawater safe to drink

- **Maths:** I think I've banged on enough about Maths, but if it's your thing, I hope you can see how the Maths can bubble to the surface in this context!

Can you identify these areas? I hope you can see others besides. There are further important elements covered as well. Can you see the possibilities for learning around the areas of:

- Compromise

- Speaking and listening

- Listening

- Team work

As well as other elements of our BRAVE curriculum? I hope so.

In this chapter, I've shown how tolerating uncertainty can actually throw up previously unseen possibilities in the directions learning can take. These learning accidents should be embraced and not seen as your lesson falling to bits.

 Signs your lesson has fallen to bits

1   Children punch the air when you fall ill halfway through teaching them

2   You rely heavily on a shared set of textbooks that the other teacher has left in their car which is getting an MOT in a garage thirty miles away

3 You really look forward to word search time which you do religiously at the end of your lesson

4 Kids don't turn up

5 You use a busy PowerPoint as a script and don't veer from it at all

6 Kids don't see the point of what you're asking them to do

7 A child threatens you with a solicitor

8 The kids have set up a petition that you know is going around the class asking for your removal whilst you are teaching them

9 You show them the first hour of *Avatar* every Friday afternoon

10 The head asks for your keys

Love the accidental moments.

Be brave.

This is all well and good, I hear you cry, but what will everyone think? There's no room for mavericks anymore! Yes there bloody is. You just don't have to shout about it. You just need to get on with it.

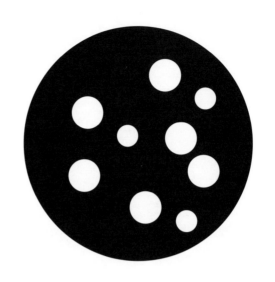

- How do we get cheese from the moon?

Inspector of the Lure

I keep six honest serving men
(They taught me all I knew);
Their names are What and Why and When
And How and Where and Who.

Rudyard Kipling

Before the class arrive at your room, grab an imaginary spade and dig a deep hole. Then, as you hear them approaching, cover the hole with vines, leaves and branches – anything your imagination can find. As the class enter, let them fall into your trap. This is essentially what we should be doing as teachers. Trapping the children into learning – hooking them in and luring them into engagement.

You'll read in Chapter 6 about how we can use technology to support learning and teaching. Here, I want look at what you need to do in order to *engage* children in what you want to teach them. If you're an experienced teacher reading this, it may mean that you need to reassess your established schemes of work (projects). If you are new to the profession, or on the outside looking in, then you will get some ideas and thinking points from what I offer. This is a serious rule of engagement: essentially how we get kids to look in our direction and listen to what we have to say. Trust me, I am an inspector of the lure (if you're under 30, you might not *get* that).

Really ace questions

A 4-year-old asks the best questions. Here are some I've heard in my house:

- How do we get cheese from the moon?

- Why do we have bones?

- Why don't penguins talk?

- Does God laugh?

I'm sure you have great examples of your own. When young children ask questions they are genuinely voicing a mystery that has emerged in their minds. They can be open questions of the highest order which require (often from a tested adult) a detailed answer which itself is open in nature. If we're feeling brave, we adults may actually respond with a question in order to continue the conversation, deepen the curiosity, build on the enthusiasm and perhaps heighten the fascination:

Son: How do we get cheese from the moon?

Dad: How do you think we get cheese from the moon?

Pause.

Son: With a ladder.

Dad: Can you draw the ladder for me?

Son draws a ladder and passes the paper over.

Son: Here you are.

Dad sees this:

H

Dad: It's only got one rung.

Son: I know. The moon isn't that far away Daddy.

All very sweet and easily translated into any classroom. The act of *effort* though is seated with the teacher/adult. Compare and contrast:

Four-year-old: How do we get cheese from the moon?

Teacher: Don't be silly.

It is so easy to stifle and slowly destroy the capacity to imagine. When a young child asks questions such as this, they are being authentic. They could as well be saying, 'Tell me the answer and I'm going to go away and think about it. I'll accept it, but I'm reflecting on it.' As teachers we need to take this responsibility of responding to questions and supporting the development of imagination very seriously.

 Reasons why imagination needs to be developed

1   James Dyson

2   Frank Zappa

3   J. K. Rowling

4   Bill Gates

5   Walt Disney

6   Charlie Chaplin

7   Kate Bush

8   Children's drawings

9   Children's stories

10   I believe the children are our future; teach them well ...

So, talking of cheese, what of the cheesy moon?

Teacher: How do you think we get cheese from the moon?

Pause.

Child: With a ladder.

Teacher: Can you draw it for me?

Child draws a ladder and passes the paper over.

Child: Here.

Teacher sees this: **H**

Teacher: Wow! It's only got one rung. I wonder if it's enough to get us to the moon.

Child ponders this.

It is fair to say that as children progress through school, many adopt what we could call a *passive imagination* which really comes to fruition at secondary level. My evidence for this is that you never get 12-year-olds asking if the moon is made of cheese. Passive imagination can be blamed on all sorts of things, from computer games all the way to paint-by-number summer blockbuster movies that don't allow any space for the imagination to take root; rather, the viewer is simply shown everything they need to see. There is no shade. Simply light and dark. Black and white. The passive imagination is reinforced by traditional teaching models where questions are asked in order to measure learning, test attentiveness and act as tent poles to a previous lesson. Compliance and passivity take hold which match the development of adolescence and the locking down of enthusiasm and excitement: 'Just tell me what I need to know in order to get my grade. I'll accept what you say as you're the one getting paid.'

The ace up a teacher's sleeve is the ability to ask *really ace questions* that unlock the passive imagination and unveil a landscape of learning hitherto forgotten by the learner.

Let's consider types of questions first of all.

High, open and fat
These questions invite interpretation; there is no preconceived response and they stimulate discussion and the bouncing of responses around the classroom. These could also be called *fishing* questions because it's as if you are casting a net in order to get lots of different types of answers. If you want to lure children into learning, these are the types of questions to use. Here are some examples:

- How can young people be convinced to get the best out of their time in school?

- What messages would you like to text your 30-year-old self?

- How can we stop hate and prejudice?

- If we needed to build a plane from scratch, what should we do first?

- Should the old workhouse building be demolished?

- What is the hardest subject in school?

Lower, closed and skinny

These questions invite non-negotiable responses and recited answers. These do have their place in a teacher's repertoire but don't often make for exciting learning experiences. These could also be called *shooting* questions because you're essentially inviting the learners to hit the bullseye with a one-shot response that is either right or wrong. Here are some examples:

• What is the name of your school?

• In what year were you born?

• What is the current number one download?

• What is the capital of France?

• What is a Manx cat?

• How do you spell 'beautiful'?

Here are some other good fishing *questions about questions*:

• What is a good question?

• Who needs to be a good questioner?

• What does a good question do?

• When are questioning skills important outside of school?

• What are we looking for when children answer questions?

 Questions I *used* to ask in my classroom back in the day

1 How are you doing?

2 Okay?

3 Got a pen?

4 Do I look like WHSmith's?

5 Do you get me?

6 Are you buzzin'?

7 Why didn't you go at break?

8 Where's your report?

9 Why are you late?

10 Have you had a haircut?

I know this is the case because a fantastic colleague of mine suggested I get a pupil to write down all the questions I would ask during a lesson on a sheet of paper for me to review at the end. That's what I did and the results are above. I should add that I still overuse number 6 but only after some ace questions have preceded it. You should try this and see if you fit in with this research that did the rounds a couple of years ago:

- 95% of all questions in a lesson come from the teacher

- The average time a teacher waits for a response is 2.7 seconds

- Most of the questions from pupils are low level (e.g. Can I borrow a pen?)

- Other questions are still only looking for low order responses reinforcing knowledge and understanding

Looking at the research and my own style of questioning, I could see that much of what I was asking was rhetorical. When I was asking a class, 'Do you get me?' (as in, 'Do you understand?'), none of them were going to put up their hands and tell me they didn't. They were passive complaints, and my questioning, although tenuously good for social health, was doing nothing to shift them from this position.

You could step up this process by asking another child to write down all the questions their peers ask. You may well find results like this.

 Questions asked by pupils in my class back in the day

1 Do we have to do this?

2 How long until break?

3 Do we have to?

4 Where did you get your tie from, Sir?

5 Can I go to the toilet?

6 Can I borrow a pen?

7 Can I go on games? (usually in a computer room with motor bike scrambling being the popular game of choice)

8 Can I go and get a hot water bottle? (always a good one to fluster young male teachers)

9 Can we pack up?

10 Can you let us out early?

Depressing reading? Try some action research yourself and see what *you* get back. If you're teaching younger children, ask your teaching assistant to help you with the experiment. Or perhaps that trainee from the local university could lend a hand. If you try it, you'll get a good barometer reading as to the state of *questioning* and *enquiry* in your classroom. Like me, you may find that you need to raise your game in terms of questioning.

Here are some reasons why questions are so important in our classrooms:

- Focus attention

- Reinforce learnt material

- Assess

- Spark further questions

- Lure students into learning

- Support evaluations of work done

- Motivate enquiry

- Identify gaps in knowledge and perception

- Encourage reflection

Ace questions also:

- Cultivate imagination

- Create a healthy learning tension

These last two points are the levers that should motivate anyone leading learning to ask better questions. The cultivation of a *flexible* imagination – one that is rich, authentic and can allow connections to be made between the world of the classroom and the real world outside – is key to growing great people. Surely we want our children and young people to be worldly wise as well as street wise? A healthy learning tension is an atmosphere where uncertainty is tolerated and judgement suspended; it is a place where silence is there to think within and where questions are used to dig deeper. These types of questions themselves can act as lures into learning. They can engage in the spirit of a problem or dilemma that needs solving where the onus of solution rests with the student. Note that the examples below are all posed in the *inductive* – that is, the teacher is *in* with the class and speaking using *we* instead of the instructional *you*.

Questions to cultivate an imaginative tension

1   If we are going to build a spacecraft to travel beyond our solar system, what's the first thing we should do?

2   What tools do we need in our kitbag that will enable us to get to the centre of the earth?

3   How can we as a class, sitting in a classroom in the middle of our town, help those in other countries who are suffering famine?

4   How can we make sure the historic mill is not torn down to make way for new houses?

5   What shall we say to the old man who needs to be moved from his house as it has become unsafe?

6   What shall we put on the signs warning people not to leave or enter our village as we're harbouring the plague?

7   What rules do we need if we are going to use the time machine we have invented?

8   What do we need to say to the Mayor to encourage him to pay the Pied Piper?

9   If we are going to rehabilitate the Big Bad Wolf, what's the first thing we need to organise?

10 How do we exhibit a gorgon?

Take a look at what you are planning to teach tomorrow. How can you look at your plan differently? You should be able to find some opportunities to ask these sorts of questions whether you're teaching measurement or the Industrial Revolution. Also, I'm sure you've noticed, these questions are all based on *contexts* – from space travel to the plague to Greek beasts. I'll say more about learning in context below.

A skilled teacher who is asking 95% of the questions in the classroom is someone who hasn't practised. Let us be clear about that. Asking really great questions doesn't just happen because you decide you're going to do it. It takes practice. And within that, initially at least, lies the need to plan your questioning.

The fabulous and much missed Ted Wragg talked about planning questions to ask in classrooms some time ago. He was one of many experts seeking to categorise and make sense of questions in the classroom. He offered a couple of ideas that are more than helpful. The first model breaks questions into three types:

1   **Empirical:** where questions require answers based on facts

2   **Conceptual:** where questions are concerned with definitions and reasoning

3   **Value:** where questions uncover moral issues and personal responses

The second model uses the joyfully appropriate acronym IDEA (Identify, Decide, Extend, Analyse), which you can utilise when planning a particular lesson. Here I'm thinking about the plague as I mentioned that topic in question 6 above.

Identify the key questions in relation to the learning intentions for the lesson:

- What was the plague?

- How did it spread?

- How was it contained?

- What were the tell-tale signs of infection?

Decide on the level, order and timing of questions:

- Look at how your questions can encourage pupil questions as well as answers

- Devote time for discussion within the plan rather than chucking in the rather useless 'Any questions?' twelve seconds before the bell goes

- Use Bloom's Taxonomy of Learning to support your planning of higher order questions or an alternative, such as SOLO (Structured Overview of Learning Outcomes – see Biggs and Collis, 1982), a system of levels enabling students to move from *pre-structural* interpretation of information to *extended abstract* uses of information. Seek it out as it's a useful alternative to Bloom's

- Think about your class and how your questions can include everyone – use your questions to differentiate *by support*

Extend the questioning by thinking of subsidiary questions to ask:

- In terms of planning, you could write your key question and then brainstorm around it. If you treat the main question as the tin can, the extended questions are the worms that come wriggling out when you open it. Here's an example:

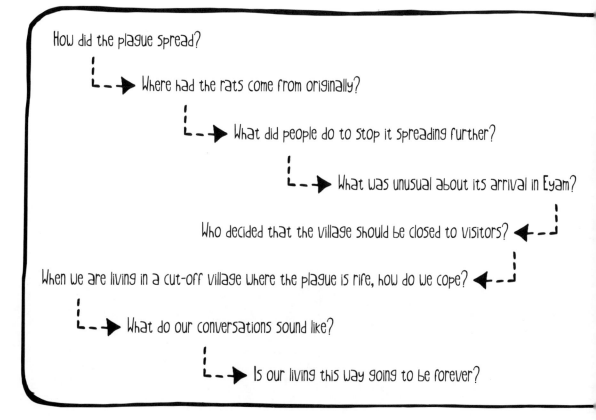

How did the plague spread?

    └─▶ Where had the rats come from originally?

          └─▶ What did people do to stop it spreading further?

              └─▶ What was unusual about its arrival in Eyam?

Who decided that the village should be closed to visitors? ◀──┘

When we are living in a cut-off village where the plague is rife, how do we cope? ◀──┘

    └─▶ What do our conversations sound like?

          └─▶ Is our living this way going to be forever?

Can you see that the questions have shifted gear as they have progressed? Also, the shift is there in terms of the inductive approach and the imaginative tension has been allowed to breathe. This sort of questioning enables a teacher to protect the class into a context for learning. More on this later.

Analyse anticipated answers and responses you might give:

- You ask your question and are able to anticipate the answer so are ready to say much more than 'well done' or 'yes, that's correct'; rather, you are ready to say

---

Well done, but have you considered that the plague was also spread by fleas living in textiles? What rules should we impose then?

Or

Yes, that's correct. So what I'm hearing you say is that we build a huge wall around the village. Are we well enough to do such manual work?

This process of answers/responses being bounced around the room, with further questions being asked by learners and teacher, can be summed up like this:

- There are a lot of planning templates out there to support teachers. One that I have been using recently is a free mind-mapping software called Spicy Nodes (www. spicynodes.org). You can use it with your class and get them to plan their own questions and encourage higher order thinking at the same time. Everybody wins. If you're struggling for Internet access in your classroom, simply use big sheets and fat pens (which encourage big ideas and fat questions)!

Blooming 'eck

I offer these models to you so you can reflect on your use of questions and any planning you might do around them. Another great tool to help you plan for questioning is Bloom's Taxonomy of Higher Order Thinking Skills which you'll either be totally familiar with, intimidated by or never heard of. The interesting thing about it is that the thinking behind this model was published back in 1956 and yet we're still using it as an analytical tool today. Using Bloom's model, questions can be categorised on six levels according to whether they test knowledge (lowest level), comprehension, application, analysis, synthesis or evaluation (highest level). Following on from Wragg's models above, you can use Bloom to plan your questions:

Knowledge

- Recalling stuff done previously – important to build on
- Who went on the bear hunt?

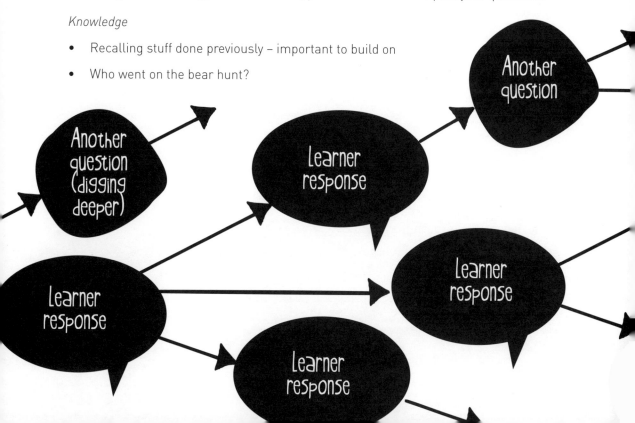

Comprehension

- Where pupils can explain their learning

- What was the weather like on the bear hunt?

Application

- Being able to use learning within a context

- In our town, where's the best place to find a bear?

Analysis

- Where learning is deconstructed

- What parts of this story can't be true?

Synthesis

- Where pupils use the learning and connect it up with other ideas

- Can you think of a different ending to the story?

Evaluation

- Comparing and contrasting new ideas with what has gone before

- How can we encourage the bear to behave? What will his behaviour plan look like?

A former student of Bloom, Lorin Anderson, reorganised the original list in the 1990s to help out teachers. It is a bit clearer perhaps so maybe you'll find it useful when thinking about your own questioning. The key change is the addition of the category *Creating* and the alteration of the other categories from nouns to verbs. So what you get is this:

Remembering
Who wrote the poem 'Storm on the Island'?

Understanding
Can you explain what the poem is about?

Applying
How does the poet demonstrate the violence of the weather?

Analysing
Do we recognise the weather described by the poet?

Evaluating
Are the people content to be battling against the weather that ravages their island?
To whom does the island belong?

Creating
How would the poet describe the island after the storm has gone?
What are the verses waiting to be written?

Cheers Lorin! That's a lot clearer! (Questions tell us a lot about the questioner, don't they.)

Reason can answer questions, but imagination has to ask them.

Dr Ralph Gerard

Eight great ways a teacher can make questions important in their classroom

1 **Teacher vocalising thinking and wonder aloud**
   I'm really wondering how we are going to convince the old lady to leave her home.

2 **Teacher fallibility**
   I really don't know the answer to this. She's lived here a long time. Do you?

3 **Teacher modelling questioning for pupils**
   The questions I have for the old lady are: Would you like to live nearer your family on the mainland? How are you going to cope on this island alone? How can we stop people worrying about you? These are my questions for the old lady when we meet her. What are yours?

4 **Teacher provides opportunities for pupils to practise their skills**

   • Use hot seating

   • Generate questions for a press conference

   • Ask pupils to prepare their own exam questions then get them to answer each other's

5   Teacher plans time for pupils' questions and for dealing with them effectively

All that planning you've done should include authentic *waiting time*. This is the sort of thing that needs to be practised (like all engagement strategies). In other words, bite your tongue.

6   Teacher uses wrong answers to develop understanding

Rather than telling Susie she's wrong, you simply ask Nigel what he has to say about her answer.

7   Teacher prompts pupils

Pupil prompting can be controlled by you acting like you're the conductor of the orchestra. Instead of music bouncing around the room, questions do. Use children's responses to your questions to feed the beginnings of a discussion. Try to build up the responses – let them harmonise and build to a crescendo ... Okay, I'll stop with the music analogy but I hope you get the picture.

8   Teacher listens and responds positively

Again, this takes practice. How many times do we finish sentences for young people? When do we simply say, 'Yes, well done' for the right answer without digging deeper? We need to ensure we don't *shut down* responses from children – opening cans of worms can offer great learning opportunities. Responding positively needs to be at the forefront of your mind and especially in the context of classroom management and positive engagement.

Here's something I saw in a secondary IT lesson recently:

Lesson: IT – Just before lunch

Class: 11- and 12-year-olds

Context: Secondary school in a tough part of town. The class were producing PowerPoints about Nelson Mandela ready for a presentation.

Basically, the class were nipping onto the Internet and copying and pasting information about Nelson Mandela (date of birth etc.) into very gaudy presentations. Now, the information being gathered here under the very close instruction of the teacher may not have been as important as the learning and understanding of Information Technology. Whatever.

In the class, there was a boy who was attempting to push the teacher's buttons. It was a classic example of a child unchallenged by the work being set. (Do we still need to have the producing of PowerPoints on the secondary curriculum when they build them so well in primary?)

The boy was using the nagging tactic often deployed by children who are bored. I then watched him get sucked into some information he'd uncovered on the Internet. I watched the reactions form on his face and then his hand go up.

This was the last straw for the teacher, sick of this annoying child:

'What?' said the teacher.

'Sir, was Nelson Mandela an activist or a terrorist?' asked the boy, staring at the screen.

'We're not doing that today! Get on with what you've been told to do!' hollered the teacher in reply.

The boy eyeballed the teacher, who had moved on to working with another group, and I could see what he was thinking.

The boy switched his computer off and slumped back in his chair, looking around for someone to kick off with. He found someone, and he did.

Nice work Teach!

Positive response is something that needs to be practised – rehearsed even – with as much effort as it takes to stamp out perceived negative behaviour. The boy in this anecdote was getting hooked into something independently, his mind cogs were racing and something had genuinely got him buzzing. He also managed to articulate a really ace question. The best, I suspect, that had been heard within those four walls for some time. With a holler, the teacher sucked the kid's enthusiasm away and the boy retreated into his predictable behaviour. Here is where the teacher *could* have gone:

- Was Nelson Mandela and activist or a terrorist?

- What do you think?

- Could we ask him?

- Should we plan what we're going to say before we meet him?

- What was it like in South Africa back then?

- Has it changed much since?

- What were the arguments for segregation?

- When we hear Nelson Mandela's story, what do we assume about the country he lived in?

And so on.

So, crates

Or, alternatively, Socrates, the ancient Greek Athenian philosopher. Apparently he once said:

An honest man is always a child.

He said lots of other things as well but never wrote any of it down. Consequently we've had to rely on his students and contemporaries – folk like Plato – to keep us up to speed with what he was about. And what he was *on* about.

If we are talking about cans of worms in terms of questioning, then Socrates and his Socratic questioning makes for an excellent can opener. Here are some examples of Socratic questioning:

- What are you assuming?

- What do you mean by that comment?

- What are your reasons for saying that?

- Are your reasons adequate?

- What effect would that decision have?

- What is the alternative?

As you can see, Socratic questions enable the simple Q&A to progress into a conversation and they are another good touchstone for us when planning questioning. You may find yourself sounding a little like a Jedi master ('Assume what, do you?' 'By that comment, what mean you?'), but this sort of questioning really does make young people think *harder* about their responses: they invite them to *elaborate*.

Celebrate good times – come on!

As a teacher it's brilliant when young people are hooked into their learning so much that they are able to articulate what they're discovering. This is true from the youngest children upwards. But how can we actually set about celebrating really ace questioning from our young people? If we feel we've used some excellent questioning techniques, drawing on Bloom's, Socrates, Wragg and other … er … blokes, then what is the evidence in the classroom? How can we demonstrate how good our young people are at creating really fab questions?

Ten ways of celebrating really ace questions in your school

1 **Question of the Week:** Coupled maybe with the Questioner of the Week. Celebrated in the form of a display on the wall, a section on the school website, a mention in assembly or (for the more reluctant pupil) a postcard home (perhaps with a picture of Socrates or Bamber Gascoigne on it).

2 **Question wall:** It's a wall. With questions on it. But hang on, there's more to it than that! For example, these are the questions the children created when they were about to meet Queen Elizabeth I. These are the questions they wanted to ask her and that

they predicted she might ask them as a visitor to the twenty-first century. These are questions the community would ask when they hear she's arrived. All on one wall. Not typed up by the teacher, but written with bad spelling and everyfing on sticky notes.

3 **Giving time:** The teacher throws out a question, fishing for responses. The hands of the enthusiastic regulars shoot up in the air. The teacher motions for them to wait. Silence is tolerated. This sounds easy, but in reality it takes a lot of practice.

4 **Regular praise:** Sometimes praise, when used too often, can become meaningless. If you keep telling a child that they're excellent when, in reality, they are simply following an instruction, you end up looking really easily pleased. And therefore a little flaky. A pushover. When a young person asks a question like

---

Was Nelson Mandela an activist or a terrorist?

---

you can afford the time to unpick the greatness of the question and back up your praise with an authentic human response, thus modelling a reaction to ace questioning.

5 **Beyond the classroom:** I recently saw a primary school dining room (i.e. the hall) where a display had been mounted for everyone to see. It was all about questioning and pupils were invited to contribute a question when they had finished eating. It wasn't formal, but the fact that it was there on show made it important. I heard a lunchtime supervisor (aka dinner lady) asking an 8-year-old how long the display was staying up. 'How long should it stay up?' came the reply. Bingo.

6 **Meaningful display:** I know I bang on about display (please see elsewhere in this book). But I will add that *meaningful* display is paramount. If you're going to do it, do it right. Don't just make a collage of Nelson Mandela pictures and facts about him up on a wall if you're doing civil rights. Dig deeper and get to the heart of the matter and use questioning as a vehicle to do so. Then bung the results up on your wall.

7 **Bathtub time machine:** Your granny's bathtub is a time machine. We can use it to travel back in time and pick up historical figures for interview and hot seating purposes. See also fast car time machine, spacehopper time hopper, wardrobe time machine and so on. You get the drift. It is a way of getting young people ready to meet someone from history and also a means for you to get these characters into your classroom. After giving time for the class to create appropriate questions, you take the role of the historical figure whilst your teaching assistant or nominated child kicks off with:

Hello. Welcome to our class. How was the bathtub?

From the jovial ice-breaking opening, the questions then move into what they should be doing – diving deeper.

8   **Assessment for Learning:** Children questioning each other about their work. Socratic questioning fits in neatly here, particularly with older pupils.

9   **Whole year assemblies:** Great questions can be the basis of great lessons, and also great assemblies. Here's a cracker:

I've been contributing to Comic Relief for years but there are still starving children on my television. Should I do something different this year?

If you're in secondary, give that to your form group to tackle. If you're in junior education, *you* take it on or slip it to the head teacher to deal with during an assembly. Children do think about stuff like this so, if you teach English or Citizenship, there's a great response somewhere waiting to be written.

10 **Google-proof homework:** A version of the above where the key question is set as a *thinking* homework. Good for readers of Jim Smith's brilliant *Lazy Teacher's Handbook* and an antidote to marking meaningless stuff you've had to set because your school has a homework policy written by people who never have to set or mark it. No need to write anything up. Simply, the question is asked and time given (see number 3 above). A lot of time. Maybe a week. Depending on the question, of course. Questions like:

- When should the police be armed?

- What things should every child have the opportunity to do before they leave school?

- Should you have a right to choose who lives in your street?

How will you know if your kids have actually done what you've asked? Well, you ask them, randomly, for an opinion.

Also, the Internet doesn't know the answer to these questions, so turn off the technology and plug in the mind. Buzzing!

Covering holes with branches or chasing the elephant

And so onto unlocking the imagination. We can use really ace questions to do this and it's important that we practise, model and reflect on the way we use questioning. After all, we want our young people to become better questioners, don't we? Being able to ask questions of those we meet – our friends, our families, our workmates, those in authority – is a genuine skill all people should be allowed to nurture, possess and share. It's not just a skill, however, it's *currency for life*.

I've mentioned elsewhere the importance of a curriculum that is relevant to the people who are immersed in it. If, for example, the school is having a lot of building work done, a teacher could ask: Where does the curriculum lie in this rebuild? Where are the learning opportunities? Similarly, if an elephant walks past your classroom window, you don't carry on banging on about the kings and queens of England. In order. By rote. You chase the elephant. Don't you? Or if you hear that a big budget Hollywood movie is being filmed down the road from your school, you don't ignore it and see it as distant and incommunicable; you get your kids to it or, better still, try to bring it into your school. Recently, a school managed to get Hollywood A-lister (at the time of writing) Johnny Depp, in full pirate regalia, into an assembly as he was shooting scenes from the latest *Pirates of the Caribbean* movie nearby. This is of course an extreme example. But if I was teaching in Manchester, I'd be looking at how a 26-minute TV programme producing three new episodes a week manages to sustain tension over such slim running time. I'd be looking at soap conventions and the reasons why such drama grips the nation in the way it does. If I worked in London, I'd do the same. Wearing an Alfie Moon shirt of course. So what's going on near you? And don't say 'nothing'.

I've spent most of my professional teaching life working in Barnsley, South Yorkshire. Here's some curriculum I've tapped into:

- The mining industry

- The demise of the mining industry

- The psychological scars on a community where the major industry has stopped

- The Silkstone mining disaster which led to a change in child labour laws in Britain at the start of the twentieth century

- *A Kestrel for a Knave* by Barry Hines

- The Barnsley Pals (the nickname for two Barnsley battalions during the First World War)

I know there's a lot of stuff about mining in this area, but hey, that's the elephant that was walking past my classroom window. So where's the curriculum here? Well, if you put mining in the context of Barnsley, at the centre of a big sheet of paper, you may find it very easy indeed to populate it with wider curriculum hits:

☑ **Geography:** industry and population

☑ **History:** mining disaster, legislation, the miners' strike, the impact and legacy of pit closure

☑ **Science:** making mines safe

☑ **English:** contemporary accounts of mining life

☑ **Mathematics:** depths of pits, distance covered, production

☑ **Art:** contemporary work by Yorkshire artists looking back at the 1980s strike

☑ **Drama:** the play of *Kes* adapted from Barry Hines' novel *A Kestrel for a Knave*

☑ **Music:** 'Between the Wars' by Billy Bragg, protest songs

☑ **Design Technology:** changes in mining technology from 1860 to the present day

☑ **MFL:** the support offered to miners from around the world, e.g. aid offered from Russia to support the strike

☑ **IT:** visual representations, backed up with appropriate soundtracks, capturing the mood of the 1980s at the closure of the industry

☑ **Citizenship:** community welfare, post-16 choice, role of education

This is just a broad example of what could be focused on. There is more to it however as I'm sure you'll appreciate. What I've listed here are either broad topics of study or actual tasks to be completed. There is an issue of coverage – for example, am I spending too much time on Drama and not enough on Mathematics? – but you are the leader of learning in your classroom. What do you want to do with your kids?

Don't panic, I'm not trying to turn you into a maverick. I do however want you to think about the curriculum you are delivering. What opportunities are you currently missing? What could you do more of? When teaching literacy, how can you include Design Technology? When delivering numeracy, how can you include Drama? It is possible, and I want to show you how.

If you look at the big sheet of paper we've created in our heads you'll see the word 'mining' in the centre with the ideas outlined above shooting out from the centre. This is all well and good. But I want to be an adventurous teacher. A teacher who inspires, engages and lures children into great learning. To do this I need to dig my hole and cover it with branches. There are a number of ways of doing this, some discussed elsewhere in this book. For example, I could get a very powerful image from the Miners' Strike of, say, a miner squaring up to a row of police officers, and we could do some powerful questioning around it – teacher-planned questions and class-generated questions. We could talk to the police officers and miners through hot seating and other dramatic conventions. We could use a powerful image to create a hot enquiry question:

Should failing industries be supported in order to sustain communities?

Or

When is it wrong to protest?

For younger children we could ask question like

Are these people happy?

Or

What can we do to make these people happy?

I saw something similar to this at an infant school where the head teacher had brought in a professional songwriter to work with the youngest children. The answer to this question was, of course, *singing*! And these children wrote the songs they wanted to sing.

After digging the hole and covering it with leaves, we could show the class appropriate clips from *Brassed Off* and *Billy Elliot*, two fine films which use the demise of the mining industry as a background to robust character study.

Yes, we could do that. My preference however is something quite different. And almost exactly the same. I would dig my hole, cover it in leaves and then stand near the front of the class, quite bemused at something in my hands.

A letter. An old letter. Probably prepared under my grill last night for reasons of authenticity.

I would have in my hands a *lure*. The thing that is going to get my class to tread on the fragile leaves.

- When can I come back in?

Room with a View

NOW, what I want is, FACTS. Teach these boys and girls nothing but Facts. Facts alone are wanted in life. Plant nothing else, and root out everything else.

Mr Gradgrind, *Hard TImes,* **Charles Dickens**

There are many perceived divisions between teaching in a primary and a secondary school. For example, there is something static and immersive about primary (or junior) classrooms. They have fixed walls that act as templates for unlocking creativity and imagination. They are places that offer sanctuary for youngsters; places where success, celebration and personality are writ large and bold. Primary classrooms really make learning matter.

In secondary (or senior) school, classrooms can often cease to be accurate reflections of the teachers who use them. They are more functional – rooms in which facts can be accessed. In our newer secondary schools, even walls can be noticeable by their absence. If you are lucky enough to have your own space in which to teach, then it's vital to ensure you are using it as the excellent resource it can potentially be.

If it's your room, what are you doing to stamp your expectations on it? If you teach in more than one room in a day, how are you making the space around you resonate with your teaching and learning style? With your personality? With your wit and wisdom?

Here are some ideas to help you answer these questions.

Clear expectations

As described in previous chapters, if you want your class engaged, your expectations need to be clear. Gone are the days of having children write down your rules in their exercise books and asking them to cover their books for homework. Do you remember that one? It was the standard first lesson for many teachers back in the day.

Children have got used to the parlance of expectation as discussed by and with their teachers. If you ask your class in that first lesson in September how they should approach their learning, they will more than likely tell you what you want to hear:

Teacher:	What are my expectations?
Pupil A:	Good listening, Miss.
Pupil B:	Hands up, Sir, when answering a question.
Pupil C:	No shouting!
Pupil D:	Walk in quietly, Miss.
Pupil E:	Settle down after playtime, Miss.

The reality is that in that first September lesson we should be agreeing ways of working, rather than just having children recite meaninglessness and second guesses. A better approach in that initial class (even with the youngest of children) is asking:

How do we want to be in this class?

Or

When we are at our best, what are we being like?

I know this may not cut the mustard with cynical senior students, but it's all in the way you *talk*. Older students will respond well to positive teacher-talk:

I really like it when you listen carefully to what I say. Is it okay if we always get our bags and coats away as fast as we can? Thanks.

Don't forget, expectations will only be met if you make them part of your everyday teacher-speak. You should even give a nod to them in your planning.

Why clear expectations are important

1 Pupils and adults need to know what is *expected* of them if they are to be successful

2 Clarifying expectations helps to create a positive atmosphere by emphasising what is *wanted* and *valued*

3 Stating specific expectations offers a framework for *explicitly identifying the behaviours you need to teach* so that all pupils have the opportunity to succeed

4 Expectations create *psychological contracts* on which to base your dealings with low-level disruption

5 Embedding clear expectations into your daily practice supports consistent engagement

The class may be the worst in their year group, but for you they work well. Other teachers who teach them may not be able to fathom it, but that's because their expectations are vague and solely based on the whole school expectations that are printed in the planner at the bottom of their bag. These teachers also have expectations around this class – but their assumption is that they will be poorly behaved and that the lesson will be a negative experience for everyone concerned. Unsurprisingly, the class live up to this expectation. Don't let that happen to you.

Measure yourself

In your mind, place yourself on this line

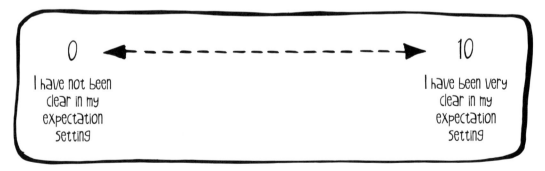

Where have you placed yourself?

Try again with this:

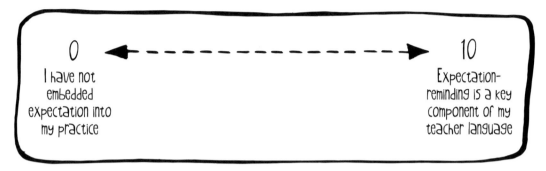

0
I have not
embedded
expectation into
my practice

10
Expectation-
reminding is a key
component of my
teacher language

Are you doing enough? If you are placing yourself towards the left of the spectrum, what are you going to do tomorrow to make a shift to the right? If you have placed yourself on the right, what do you need to do to go *beyond* the 10 score? How can you turn it up to 11 (in the style of Spinal Tap)? If you have expectations but the children don't respond to you, have a look at the way you are 'selling' these expectations and listen to your own teacher-talk. If you sound depressed and cynical when attempting to embed your expectations, your children will not be inspired. And that isn't rocket science, is it?

A teacher of 8-year-olds recently told me of her trouble with settling her class down after lunch. They were piling into the classroom and would take fifteen minutes or so to truly calm down. All the time she would be battling with them to quieten down in order to complete the register. This had been going on since she had taken over the class earlier in the academic year.

It's clear that the children had an expectation that the post-lunchtime session was always going to be bonkers and the teacher had the expectation that she was going to have her stress levels upped and chaos would reign until administration was finished and *real* work could begin. It turned out that the children would only settle at this point. The solution here was simple. The teacher was reinforcing one of the previous teacher's expectations by picking up where (s)he had left off. The children were behaving for their current teacher in exactly the same way they had behaved for their previous one. The teacher was being *consistent* in promoting another teacher's unsuccessful expectations. What needed to happen here was an *expectation ad campaign*. In the same way that global companies market brands all around the world, this teacher needed to do a rebrand of expectations in the world of her classroom.

Rebranding your expectations

- Give explicit descriptions of the behaviour you and your colleagues require

- Clarity: use precise language

- Involve pupils

- Involve support from colleagues as necessary (e.g. ask the head teacher to pop in to ask the class how the new expectations are going) – this may sound daft but the children, be they infants or seniors, will see that you are being serious about the issue

- Develop class behaviour plans that will underpin the expectations you establish (e.g. use seating plans and stick with them). Have a different seating plan in the morning and afternoon if you're in primary. Be creative in secondary: have several configurations of tables and vary work partners by using inside/outside – when working in *inside* groups, pupils are choosing their groups so they are warm and welcoming; *outside* groups are when pupils work in groups you've created, so they need to prepare for varying elements and negotiate unpredictables

- Turn your new expectations into displays, placemats, posters and so on – much like McDonald's does when it introduces a new burger to the market, except with less cheese and minus a scary clown

Embedding fresh expectations

- Develop and use a script which is consistent each time you use it so that the pupils become familiar with your *prompt words* (e.g. think, listen, reflect, talk, question, dig deeper, look, focus, imagine – I know these are obvious, but how often do we use them?)

- Explain the positive consequences if the pupils get it right (e.g. reward): *If we can get this done, I'll be really pleased. I'll be putting a note in your planner and seeing your form tutor*

- Explain the negative consequences if they don't get it right (e.g. sanction): *If we can't get this done, I'll be really disappointed. I'll be putting a note in your planner and seeing your form tutor*

- Being *consistent* is absolutely vital when embedding expectations. You need to reflect and check yourself because if you're not careful you can fall into the trap of a rule for one and a different rule for another. Basically, the 'naughty' kids need to see that you are not reticent in using sanctions with the 'good' kids. That's what being consistent is. It's also being fair

- Draw on your teacher repertoire around classroom management to promote these fresh expectations

 Great expectations for primary and secondary

1 We are always polite

2 We listen when asked

3 We endeavour to do the best we can

4 When the bell sounds, we shift into learning

5 We always try to get ourselves unstuck

6 We respect our learning space

7 We don't chew gum

8 We use thinking time appropriately

9 We have fun

10 We celebrate success

So how are these great expectations reinforced?

1 We are always polite

- Words like 'please' and 'thank you' are on display (laminate some onto A3) and you point at them to reinforce them

- You model politeness by being polite and not a shouty, negative monster (even though you may feel that inside)

- You meet and greet children when they come in and you wish them well when they leave – whether they're 4 or 14 – because you are a model of politeness

2 We listen when asked

Use a script that emphasises listening as a focusing tool. Have an A3 picture of an ear (or 'lug' as we say in Barnsley) on the wall that can be pointed at when you want your class to settle. Try to avoid referring to the children as:

- *Guys* (you're not an American, unless of course you are, in which case, well done and I'm pleased the book is out there)

- *Folks* (your class will think you are ancient)

- *Ma hood/posse* (avoid being *down wiv the kids* at all costs – they may like it initially but eventually they will think you're a fool and take you to the cleaners)

Try instead to use the actual name of the class, as in 'Morning Emerald Class', or specific table names as in 'I'm really impressed with Dolphin table's listening today'. Recently I heard that referring to a group of children as *people* works well as a method of focusing attention. I tried it with a senior class I was working with, as in

---

Look at me now people. Thank you.

It worked well. See if it works for you.

3   We endeavour to do the best we can

By knowing children's names, you can personalise your inputs to the class. In primary you've got no excuse not to know children's names, unless you're on supply. If you are on supply, or are just filling in for another colleague, have some stickers in your bag so kids can write their names on them and put them on their jumpers. Problem solved. Also, prior to the class, if you've time, ask for a seating plan.

In secondary knowing names can be quite a challenge, particularly if you teach a non-core subject where you see the young people just once a week or even once a fortnight. You may teach around 120 different pupils every day. Use the stickers as described above as a starting point. Seating plans also support the learning of names. If you struggle to get names embedded in your mind, get the children to help you – make it obvious you are endeavouring to do your best. They will appreciate it. Another way of getting names embedded in your brain is to access the school's mugshots of the children you teach. Stick them into your planner. Do it in September and you shouldn't need them by November.

4   When the bell sounds, we shift into learning

Many schools have dispensed with the school bell as it often simply signalled the beginning of chaos! Learning starts and ends on *your* signal. If your signal is not clear, expect a messy start to your lesson. The boisterous junior class described earlier were slow to settle because the teacher was slow to get them focused. What is your signal that learning is beginning and ending? Remember, children don't think in terms of three-part lessons!

5   We always try to get ourselves unstuck

Education experts Dylan Wiliam and Paul Black unleashed the principles and practicalities of Assessment for Learning on an unsuspecting profession back in 1998 in their publication *Inside the Black Box*. Many of their tools and strategies have been embraced by teachers around the UK and beyond as methods of engaging children and young people in improving their work through a *learning dialogue*. Assessment for Learning places the teacher inside the action instead of having them remain as the *sage on the stage*. Being the *guide on the side* encourages learning dialogues and enables children to dig deeper into the tasks they are negotiating and allows them to articulate their reactions to the work they're doing. Here are some ideas to support kids who are just plain stuck:

- **SNOT:** ask your**s**elf, a **n**eighbour, an**o**ther adult, then, finally, the **t**eacher

- **C3B4Me:** not a *Star Wars* droid, but a message: ask three other people before you ask the teacher

Turn these two ideas into posters for your classroom. Point at them when your regular groupies are approaching you with their work! Go to www.glogster.com or www.piclits.com to make them look really good.

6   We respect our learning space

Put simply, don't allow anyone to wreck your room. Even if it's not yours. At the end of each lesson, if there's a mess, get it tidied ready for the next class. Model this to the children and they'll follow you:

Can we just get the chairs and tables straightened up for the next class? Thanks.

Don't put up with graffiti – if it's a problem, stick some sugar paper up on the wall and let the children add their tags (nickname signatures that have a hieroglyphic look) to it. Let them get it out of their system. When they leave, get a picture of it or file it away. If any of those tags make an unwelcome appearance in your room or around the school, you'll have an idea of who the culprit is. Bless 'em.

7   We don't chew gum

Chewing gum can be the bane of a teacher's life and dealing with young people who sit there chomping like grazing sheep could warrant a chapter of its own. Briefly, it makes a mess. Once the flavour fades, kids want rid – often on the seat of a chair. Cue meltdowns from your next class when one of them gets it all over their new trousers.

8   We use thinking time appropriately

Learning in our classrooms wants to have pace, but that doesn't mean we need to bulldoze through things. As trainee teachers we are taught to reflect; we need to teach young people to do the same and give them the time and space to do so. If we want to nurture young people who are thoughtful and reflective then we need to teach them the importance of *measured thought*. We are hopefully in the business of getting our youngsters literate in various ways – digital, visual, media, textual – and we also need to support them in their development of thinking so they can move from offering low order knee-jerk responses to higher order responses which may open up the thinking of others as well as their own. This takes time.

Try one of these to get you going:

- Get a *thinking beanbag* and plonk it into your role-play area

- Create a *thinking step* for kids to use – they can sit on it, stand on it, lean on it, etc.

- Help them to think by placing *prompt questions* on the wall

- Brand up a *thinking zone* – have it as a circle of gaffer tape on the floor that the child can stand/sit in. Resist the temptation to turn it into a punishment!

- Use notes or online sticky note programs such as www.wallwisher.com to capture young people's measured reactions to challenges

- Wait for answers to your questions. We often give groups time to plan for presentations – do we give individual children the same opportunity? It goes back to what I've already mentioned about questioning: ask the question, then wait, wait, wait! And then, wait a little longer!

- If it's first thing in the morning and you've got a form group, get them thinking straight away by putting a philosophical statement up on the board. Tell them you'll ask them for their responses to the statement later in the session. Here are some examples:

» Being happy is more important than being rich

» Don't miss the doughnut by looking through the hole

» If you chase two rabbits, you won't catch either one

» Eggs cannot be unscrambled

» A stumble may prevent a fall

» When you throw dirt, you lose ground

» It isn't what you know that counts, it's what you think of in time

» Just remember, there's a right way and a wrong way to do everything and the wrong way is to keep trying to make everybody else do it the right way (this one is from the TV show *M*A*S*H* as spoken by the wizened Colonel Potter)

Also, buy a copy of *The Little Book of Thunks*® by Ian Gilbert and you'll find a book full of ace head-scratchers.

9   We have fun

Children define engagement as fun. I'm trying to help with this book.

10 We celebrate success

• It's important to remember that even older students enjoy celebrations of success. You don't need to put their name into a raffle to win a BMX at the end of term. You can just try saying, 'Well done Josh. That was awesome.' If you've invested in relationships, it'll save you a few hundred quid at Halfords

• Celebration features as part of your display – see below

• We celebrate subtly as well as overtly: a whisper in the ear to one child is a shout from the mountaintops to another

In this rundown of potential expectations, I hope you've noticed the word *we* – these expectations are for you as well. You need to model these expectations in order to embed them. Here's another list of expectations we used in my school when we ran a fresh and innovative blended curriculum for 11- to 13-year-olds.

• I commit

• I communicate

• I collaborate

- I concentrate
- I consider and am considerate
- I create

This list was created by the staff who were going to be running the innovative curriculum prior to its launch the following autumn. During those planning sessions we were keen for the children to have clear expectations of how we would work and the *frame* in which the collected 'we' would operate. These expectations, and this manifesto, was then the basis of the first couple of weeks of teaching when the classes arrived in September.

In primary phase you could perhaps use something like this:

Responsible

Enthusiasm

Action

Creative

Have a go!

Broken down, these terms can be defined like this:

Responsible

- I manage myself well
- I'm happy to be here
- I know what to do when I'm stuck
- I can motivate myself

Enthusiasm

- I'm ready to learn
- I know how I like learning best
- I can take risks
- I'm adaptable

Action

- I can manage distraction
- I can focus
- I can work well with others
- I can manage information

Creative

- I can ask great questions
- I can make links between the classroom and the world outside
- I enjoy challenge
- I enjoy stories

Have a go!

- It's okay to make mistakes
- I'm an explorer
- I listen and react positively
- I'm up for it!

Other acronyms are available. They really are surprisingly effective in terms of embedding expectations. You can slap them on your walls and use them to support your management of the classroom. They offer an anchor for you and your pupils on which to hang your shared expectations.

Display as a lure to learning

Classroom walls are points of reference for children. During examinations, assessments and tests, children's eyes lift to the wall display that explains *generic features of great creative writing*. Because of the exams, the display is now covered with blank sugar paper so the kids can't cheat. They still look though. The teacher has spent weeks referring to the display on the wall and now it's as if the children have developed x-ray vision: they see through the sheet and remember the help and support the teacher has given them. A memory of the display plays back in their young minds and they use that memory to help them produce great writing. In secondary, this process is called *revision*.

Display is to the teacher what the saw is to a carpenter: essential.

 Things to remember about display

1 Display should carry meaning to those who look at it

2 Display isn't the job of the teaching assistant, although they can help you out with it

3 Display is a reflection on you – what do your walls say about you?

4 Display needs to be managed in the same way you'd manage a flower arrangement

5 Display can be personalised using photographs of pupils

6 Display can be used to celebrate success

7 Display can be put anywhere

8 Display should stimulate enquiry and be challenging

9 Display should show processes as well as final and best pieces of work, but shouldn't be dated

10 It is often ignored – by everyone

This, of course, is all well and good but how can we make display important? We know *why* it's important, but what can we tap into to give us a helping hand?

Here are some ideas to consider that I used when I had a form group who I saw every day.

- If you've a form group or are with a class all day, dedicate some space to celebration of things done outside of school. Include yourself in this. Get a picture of that bungee jump you did up on the wall!

- You've got a girl in your class who fronts a band – put up details of where their latest download is available from

- Best new movie at the flix

- Question of the Week – speaks for itself I hope

- Questioner of the Week – see above

- Pupil mugshots backed with Velcro that can be moved in and out of a 'winners' section

- Get down to the video shop (if you've still got one near you) and ask for their movie-promotion cast offs 'for educational purposes' – for a while I had a life-size *Ocean's Eleven* cut-out welcoming people into my room

- Stick a poster up – a colleague of mine had Yoda from *The Empire Strikes Back* on which he'd put a speech bubble 'Learn You Will'. If nothing else, it got the kids engaged with him in conversations about the merits of *Star Wars*, Jedi knights and the importance of learning

You can get the kids to 'manage' the space. Make displays big and colourful. Don't be boring. Use technology to help you. Like a camera. Or the Internet.

Which brings me to how the Internet can help us in our rooms.

Technology

Remember: there was probably a time when the humble HB pencil was viewed as cutting-edge technology.

Five examples of old technology in the classroom

1   **Banda machine:** a primitive photocopier that gave off an intoxicating aroma

2   **Paper register:** I worked in a school recently where I had to do an electronic *and* paper register

3   **The floppy disk:** some schools still have IT gear with floppy disk drives on them. Still useful then, I guess

4   **Handwritten worksheets:** I made a lot of these early doors, but there's no reason to have them in this day and age

5   **Overhead projector and acetate:** I've used an overhead projector for years as a really useful spotlight when doing monologue work in Drama. That's it. You've got whiteboards now

Sigh. And now I shall go and date this book by talking about technology.

In terms of technology, this is what you need to know: the children hold the expertise. Do not pretend you know technology better than they do. Most importantly, even if you have a degree in Information Technology and Binary Algorithms, even if you are a webmaster and writing a blog regularly ... you still don't know jack.

 Things about technology that keep me awake at night

1   A 19-year-old created Facebook

2   Pupils were into Bebo whilst I was grappling with an electronic register

3   Bebo and Myspace: these one-time sensations are in decline today as the cruel short shelf life of technology kicks in

4   I discover something new every time I go online – brilliant and frightening

5   I have to write about technology in this book – turn to the back pages to find a list of my top ten websites as of today

Technology for engagement

And this is the sticky bit. You can be a technical wizard, have Flip cameras coming out of your ears and handle an interactive whiteboard with ease, but if you can't make the link between snazzy gizmos and *authentic learning*, then you're in trouble. You may as well jack it in.

Think of the Wizard in *The Wizard of Oz*. He engages (and, to be fair, frightens) Dorothy and her pals during their first meeting with his shocking technicolor display of magical wonder. However, later in the film, during the second lesson, he's revealed as the shallow charlatan he is. By a dog.

As a teacher, you can't let the technology do the work for you. Others may disagree with that. But what is important is that we shouldn't let technology wag the dog. It is brilliant to have access to outstanding e-resources like those I've listed, but as I said earlier, nothing will replace *you* and your ability to *hook* and *lure* children into genuine learning.

You may well end up in a department that gives you all the schemes of work in the form of PowerPoints on a pen drive.

I know. You may have to read that sentence again.

I've seen it in a History department where every lesson was delivered through the lens of a PowerPoint (PPT). Any magic around the awe and wonder of History was sucked away by this vampiric vehicle that essentially told the teacher what to say and directed the kids on what to think. Don't get me wrong, I quite like PPT (and its flashier friend www.prezi.com) and can see how it's an appropriate boon at times; however, it shouldn't be more than a support to your teaching. It shouldn't be the replacement for you, your skill and your knowledge. There's also something passionless about it. You might as well use a textbook.

As discussed elsewhere, if you're a teacher in a team, experienced or novice, ensure you bring the right balance of technology know-how and excellent subject knowledge to the department. If you just focus on the technology, you'll enjoy credibility currency from your colleagues for a while, but it will wane as soon as they discover you don't value the pedagogy of engagement – or, put another way, the kids take you to the cleaners. During a power cut.

I went through a stage of regularly getting taken to the cleaners by a Drama class full of 13- and 14-year-olds, a rum bunch who would spill into my classroom following break time. There were twenty-eight of them, of whom three liked the subject. I needed something to help me get them sorted. I had no desks, a slow computer on which to upload the class register and the theme of poverty to explore, with children, many of whom were living in poverty themselves. I was saved by an online image search: *rich poor contrast*. The image showed two communities existing side by side, one affluent, one poor. The image was arresting. It stopped the children in their tracks. It made them want to ask questions.

When my Drama class saw this picture, they couldn't believe it was real. After talking with them for around twenty minutes, I realised we all still had our coats on. This was my template hook for the rest of the year. An arresting image that would engage, stimulate and fascinate.

Online eye candy

Stick these into your image search engine and see if there are any diamonds that would be good to hook in a class. Images can be brilliant as a tool of engagement and as carriers of meaning. Just make sure you've got your safe search settings switched on. Particularly if you type in 'online eye candy' (who I think has her own site these days).

1   Unusual pictures

2   Laughing animals

3   Metaphor photography

4   Optical illusions

5   Fabulous landscapes

6   Album covers

7   Space

8   National Geographic

9   Amazing buildings

10 Shark helicopter

At the risk of being burned as a Luddite, may I offer the following list as a reflection on technology:

My favourite technology for learning

1   Fat pens (various colours, all working)

2   A roll of lining paper from the clearance bucket at B&Q

3   Sticky notes

4   Images (stick a load on a pen drive = instant portable resource; great if you're a cover supervisor – see above)

5   A smile

6   Some really fat and juicy questions filed in a box in your head

7   A willingness to engage the senses

8   A whiteboard that is used *interactively*

9   Music

10 A sense of humour

Just as an aside:

 Things to remember when talking to a good IT technician

1   They are an expert at what they do

2   They are your guide to a world you are constantly trying to keep up with

3   They can be shy

4   Act enlightened when the technician begins helping you, saying things like 'Oh right, yes, I see now'

5   Be prepared for no human reaction on any level from the technician

6   Focus on what is being done. Do not under any circumstances get on with something else, like teaching kids. They won't like that

7   Say a big thanks. Mean it

8   When the job is done, shake your head in disbelief and mutter words like 'Amazing'

So that's 'Room with a View'. You may wonder why technology ended up in this section. The reason is because technology should be part of the furniture of your classroom. It's as important as a chair or a table. And you should be able to cope without it should you need to.

- Children are protected into learning to ride a bike.

OR Safety First (then frighten the hell out of them!) ...
OR Protection into Learning

Leave the Baggage by the Door

A turtle makes progress when it sticks its neck out.

Anon.

Learning to ride a bike brings with it so much independence that almost every kid wants to do it as soon as possible. Toddlers learn that when you push or pull something, it moves. They have control over it. Then it's tryke-time and they learn mobility. As they get bigger, so does their vehicle of choice.

Eventually you have a bike with stabilisers – you don't automatically progress from tryke to bike, you have to go through, what can be for some, quite a steep learning curve.

When watching their child zoom along on stabilisers, parents 'ooh' and 'ahh' at the progress their child is making until the time comes for the support wheels to be removed. In some households this is such a big deal it's a ritual. The parent removes the stabilisers, holds them aloft and says, 'Never again shall these wheels be seen on your bike. They shall be cast aside as childish and banished to that shelf at the back of the shed!'.

Well, that's what happened in our house.

In reality, the stabilisers come off and are replaced, albeit briefly, by the support of the parent, clutching the seat as their child grapples with steering, direction, choices, camber and appropriate breaking. Soon, after tumbles, scrapes and grazes, the child discovers their previously hidden ability. It hasn't just been suddenly revealed, but in fact has been carefully nurtured and grown. And then, for a while at least, through the eyes of the cyclist, the world suddenly seems a little more accessible and uncomplicated.

Now everyone who has ever ridden a bike is, at this point in cycling-development, faced with a choice:

Do I carry on riding my bike and enjoying it for what it is: a means of transport?

or

Do I become an Olympic speed racer?

or

Do I wish to master the art of urban freestyle cycling?

This, of course, is all up to the cyclist themselves. Not their parents or their teachers. Just them.

I'll stop banging on, but you'll hopefully see what I mean. Children are *protected into learning* to ride a bike. They don't sit in a room and look at diagrams of wheels, chains and pedals – they get on it and pedal.

Ten ways we protect children into learning

1 When teaching children to swim we've stopped the archaic practice of throwing them in the canal

2 When teaching toddlers to hold cutlery, we pick it up for them when they drop it

3 We constantly remind crawling babies not to go near the fireplace/iron/volcano

4 We modify our language and remove cluttersome words so as to be absolutely clear. So when addressing a toddler, we say 'No! Hot!' and make the appropriate hand and facial gestures (which is why Drama is so important!), rather than say, 'No! The temperature of that oven-front is 225 degrees and will take your skin off and melt your eyeballs if you touch it! Beware!'

5 The use of sarcasm. Young people think they're great at it. Only looking back as adults will they realise they weren't. When a young person sarcastically says 'This is interesting' (meaning 'This is boring'), I respond with 'Cheers, I've spent ages putting it together!', thus diffusing their attempt at sarcasm. A sarcasm expert would reply to me with something along the lines of 'Great use of your time', and I would respond with ... and so on. But not most young people. If you're clever in diffusing their sarcasm, they'll shut up. Everyone wins. And by everybody winning I mean the other thirty kids in your class

6 When learning a musical instrument, children are given the instrument to hold – to get a feel of physically before they attempt to negotiate it musically. I was in a primary school recently where every 7-year-old child learns the violin. Fair play to the teachers there! The children explore the instrument physically before they play a note. They learn the geography of the instrument, the history of it and the science. How does rubbing horsehair across catgut create music? What's interesting here is that the children aren't sat down and taught how to correctly draw a treble clef on a stave and where middle 'C' sits. They hold the violin and play with the bow. A cacophony of learning, adventure and experiment

7 We give little girls and boys footballs and see what happens. The off-side rule comes in much later. For the boys at least

8 We read to children before they read to us. We then set them free into the world of literature

9 When a little boy is attempting to explain the plot of *Star Wars* to you, you are patient with him even though you know he is mixing up the Jawas with the Sand People. You set him straight, mind you, so that this mistake doesn't get embedded. But you let him tell the story in his own words. Eventually, he will get it right. Learn, he will

10 When setting up the popular board game Mousetrap, one of the instructions says: 'You should get an adult to help you with this bit'. It's a familiar instruction found everywhere from CBeebies to Lego

Then they come to school and we drop them straight into the Egyptians even though they've not had any breakfast. Or we throw them headlong into the Victorians even though they didn't sleep at home last night because social services are involved with the family. Or we catapult them straight into algebra even though they just don't see the point of it now that they've been moved into your set. The bottom set? Algebra? No thanks. Not unless you can make it relevant.

In the context of the classroom, the idea of protecting children into learning is one that we all should consider. Look at what you're teaching next week. How can you help your classes get *into* the learning you need them to do? Really ace questioning is one ingredient you will definitely need. But what else?

Here's an illustration of how I see this concept of *protection into learning*:

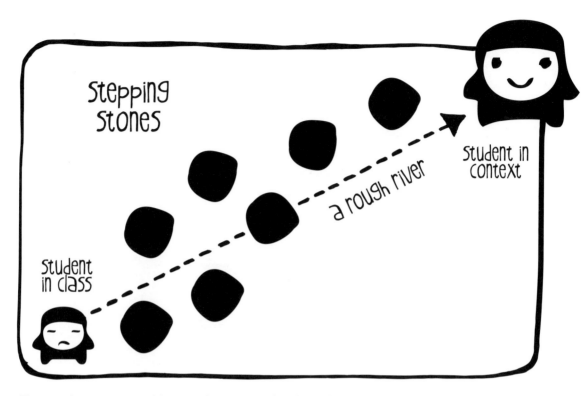

The teacher must provide stepping stones for the children to move across in order to be immersed and involved in the class work, whatever that might be. Dorothy Heathcote calls this 'lifting the mist' where clarity is achieved through a learning journey as though, at the start, a mist clouds our vision. As we progress, the mist is lifted and understanding and clarity are revealed, whilst further, perhaps more complex, questions are generated.

The stepping stones in my illustration may include classroom management elements such as clear expectations, seating plans and other absolute givens for good learning and teaching. The rough river represents the baggage, both literal and metaphorical, that children often walk into a classroom with. If Catherine has been told off at break time and given a detention, then she'll walk into your classroom with that baggage. If Darren's grandparent is seriously ill in hospital, that's his baggage. We need to be sensitive to all this whilst perhaps not needing all the details. The stepping stones support the children across this rough river.

By the time they're across, the baggage has been boxed up and left on a shelf for collection later. The business of the day has suckered them in, they have fallen through your branches and are ready to work within a context and learn some stuff.

Here's an example of how this could happen. I often use this to illustrate to teachers the concept of protecting into role. It is basically three stepping stones that get the kids hooked in. The stepping stones here can be used as a template for the work you want to get kids hooked into tomorrow.

Continuing the theme of mining used elsewhere in the book, the stepping stones are based on the story of the Chilean miners who, you may recall, were trapped underground in 2010 for more than two months until their dramatic rescue, witnessed by millions around the world. This has provided an excellent elephant walking past the window opportunity.

I most recently used this process with a mixed ability class of 11- and 12-year-old children in a school in Doncaster, South Yorkshire – a place with great mining heritage. I had a morning to take the children across the rough river, from one point (being in the room) to another (wishing to dig deeper – pun intended – into the focus (more on this later)).

The school had been experimenting with a blended curriculum, so my focus was History, Geography, Religious Education and Citizenship. In three hours this is what I did:

- I gathered the thirty-one children to the front of the classroom

- I asked them if they were *yes* or *no*. Fortunately, they were yes

- We huddled together at the front of the class. I asked them what it was like to be crushed together like this, hoping one of them would mention cramped spaces. Like caves. Or mines. In Chile

- One stuck his hand up and said 'It's like being in the lunch queue!' The others nodded in agreement

- I was patient. 'What else?' I asked, hopefully

- 'It's like being at the football.' We all swayed and cheered at an imaginary goal. (At this point Jordan and Josh started making their presence felt and I knew I'd have to deal with them shortly. Nothing bonkers. Just low level stuff)

- Then a little voice: 'Sir, it's like being on the London Underground.' We all looked at the speaker, astounded. She had been to London!

I realise that this passage across the water isn't working. I ask them to return to their seats. As they do, another girl proclaims the magic words:

It's like them miners.

- Bingo! As the class settle I enquire more about 'them miners', taking the stance of total obliviousness. I know a bit about the miners who've been trapped but don't really know a lot

- A can of worms opens. Their expertise pours out. Jordan and Josh (my very own Little and Large) join in with their detailed conspiracy theories about the miners having discovered gold but are keeping it a secret from the authorities (or something), and there is some hilarity around the fact that lovers as well as wives were turning up to witness the men being rescued

- Everyone in the class knows elements of the story and is captivated by it. Using their enthusiasm, I harness their engagement and we *go for it*

Step 1

- Day 14: first contact phone call

- Paired conversation between a miner and someone on the surface – it could be a friend, wife, girlfriend, boss, president

This got the class hooked in totally. A bit of play. For me, it's protection into learning. Once they'd had a few minutes trying out conversations, holding their telephone hands to their ears, they wanted to show what they had done. This is the challenging part for any teacher. There had been much laughter and there is a part of you that wants to stop the children and say:

Listen. You are not taking this seriously enough. Now do it again properly.

As hard as it is, this needs to be resisted. The laughter, the flowing energy, the enthusiasm, the experimentation and the engagement need to be allowed. It's part of the protection. So step back and let the children enjoy what they're doing.

So the kids are laughing and want to perform their little dialogues. By the way, I've not told them I'm a Drama teacher and I haven't said anything about 'making up plays'. I just asked them to have a conversation.

Of course Jordan and Josh wanted to show theirs. And they did. And it was funny. Not because they were using satire or being childish. It was funny because they were so into it. And using their absolutely authentic South Yorkshire accents. It was brilliant. I'd keep my eye on them, but for now, J+J were hooked. Through the branches and down the hole.

Moving on ...

Step 2

- Before long, a tube the width of a drainpipe connects the miners with the world
- Create an object of hope that can be sent down the pipe

The laughter and hilarity (embarrassment and bemusement?) from Step 1 evaporated here as the class wanted to move on with another focus. The concept of an *object of hope* was easily catered for in the preamble discussion before I let them go. They came up with:

- Photographs of family members
- Recordings of messages sent on MP3 devices
- Letters
- Cards

Great ideas in themselves, but the well, as they say, was getting dry, until a bespectacled lad at the front asked a beautiful question:

Can we invent something that's never been invented before?

(Hang about! This is senior school! We don't do this sort of thing. We've got this scheme of work to follow ...) I replied:

Of course.

What you have to understand is that for a secondary teacher that simple response takes some strength and bravery. It symbolises the 'letting go' I talked about earlier. I'm allowing the imaginative and creative leanings that all children possess to take over. I'm sweating, when, almost immediately, Jordan shouts:

We can do a *Dragons' Den*!

To cut to the chase: the sugar paper and fat pens came out and the class were suddenly preparing pitches for a *Dragons' Den* type arrangement where Jordan and Josh were taking the roles of the Dragons! Whilst the rest of the class were creating their objects of hope, these two were creating their respective curricula vitae to back up their credentials for taking on such high-powered roles. (The observing class teacher later commented that the boys wrote more during this task than they had done since the start of term.)

Here are some of the ideas that were shared when the class were called back together:

- An inflatable sofa
- A hat with inbuilt head-massager
- A deflated football and a pump
- Virtuosity Glasses that when worn visualise your home, friends and family

A quiet girl at the back had simply drawn a flower to send down. 'It'll dee (die)!' shouted Jordan (bless him). Fast as lightening, she retorted:

I'm going to send down a fresh one every day.

Jordan simply nodded in acceptance. I don't think the girl would normally have stood up to this larger-than-life character, but she was increasingly enveloped within this safe haven of learning. It was okay for her to bounce back at him. I loved it.

There wasn't much time left and I was keen to get to what was (in my head) the final stepping stone:

Step 3

- Write a letter of inspiration and reassurance from the miners to the people wishing to rescue them

Please note what I have done here: I've dragged the kids underground. Remember the laughter and hilarity from Step 1? That was gone. It had been replaced by a commitment to the work being done. There was something else as well: a commitment to me. Writing the letter described here is the toughest thing I'd asked the class to do. We had a preamble discussion which covered:

- What do we want to say?

- Who do we want to read the letter?

- What do we want them to feel when they read our letter?

- How can we sound calm and positive?

- What language can we use to be inspiring and reassuring?

Scraps of paper out. Not a word was spoken and the children wrote their letters. I hadn't talked them through the conventions of writing a letter – it was their human reaction *in role as a miner* that was more important than structures.

I checked the clock and lunch was looming heralding the close of the session. I got the class huddled to the front as we had been at the start of the lesson. I whispered to them:

Let's hear the letters before we send them up.

Each child had a letter. Most of them read theirs out. Some chose not to and, do you know what, that's fine. Josh's letter finished with:

I can't wait to see you again. My eyes are tired without you.

Hold you soon,

Josh

The letters were left on the desk at the front and the bell went. That was it. Off to lunch. Off to get some baggage. But, and make no mistake, this class was buzzing and ready to pick up what was coming next lesson. Trouble is, in senior (or secondary) school, next lesson can mean next week, but that's another issue.

The children left. Their regular teacher was pleased as I had met the objectives she'd set out for me during our initial planning discussion. I hadn't shared them with the class. And I haven't shared them with you yet! Be clear on this: every time you stand in front of a class, you need to know what your objectives are. You absolutely need to know what the children in your care will be learning. Nobody can 'wing it' even if they think they can.

Here are the objectives I'd been asked to meet:

- To give pupils freedom to explore and be creative, individually and in small groups

- To produce a short piece of writing that can be used as a springboard to further work

- To protect the learners into a project on child labour

What happened next when the real teacher took over

The teacher was focusing on two events:

- Huskar Mining Disaster at Moor End Colliery, Silkstone, Barnsley, 1838

- Cadeby Main Colliery Disaster at Conisbrough, near Doncaster, 1912

She was keeping her options open in terms of these two local events. The class looked into the 1912 event first and considered how the centenary of the disaster should/could be remembered. For this, the class became local historians for some of the time and professional organisers of events for the rest.

The other event, the Huskar Mining disaster of 1838, was very significant in terms of changing the laws around children working down mines. A violent storm caused the pit to flood drowning twenty-six children, the youngest just 7 years old, the eldest 16. Queen Victoria demanded a public inquiry which sat for three years. The report that came from the inquiry led to the passing of the Coal Mines Act in 1842, which resulted in the raising of the minimum age of working child miners to 10 years of age. For this element the teacher was going to work with the class on building a series of eyewitness accounts. She was then going to bring the class bang up to date with a return to the story of the Chilean miners, but not before looping the idea of Huskar's child workers with those children working in the diamond mines of Africa and India today.

To illustrate a learning journey, how about this:

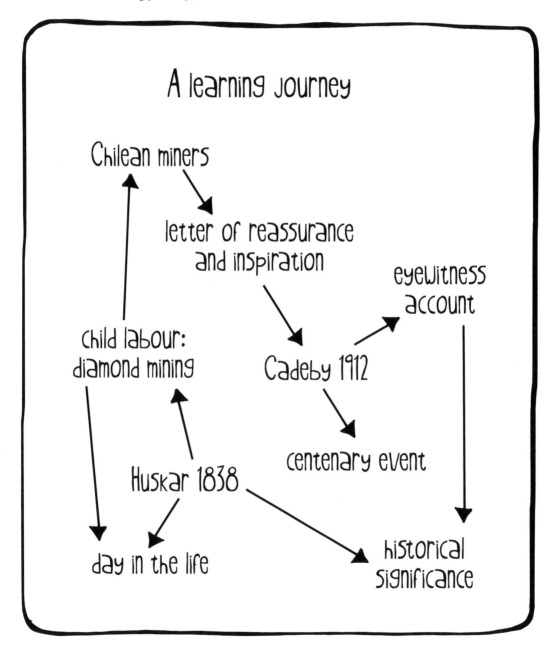

You can hopefully see how the contemporary elephants outside the window (the Chilean miners, mining industry, Third World child miners) have been used to inform the study of History. The child labour aspect of this work was important to the teacher as she felt the class needed to have more understanding and empathy with children of their own age in other parts of the world. The Chilean miners' story was a lure to get them to that position.

Where does the curriculum lie in the story of the Chilean miners?

- **Geography:** where did it happen? Is this the area's main industry?
- **History:** mining disaster, legislation, the miners' strike, the impact and legacy of pit closure
- **Science:** making mines safe, rescuing the Chilean miners
- **English:** news reports
- **Mathematics:** measuring the length of the pipe that would be needed to ferry the miners to the surface
- **Art:** designing a sculpture that could commemorate the rescue and the story of the men
- **Drama:** leaving home for the shift prior to the disaster, interviews
- **Music:** celebration song commemorating the rescue
- **Design Technology:** scale model of rescue pod
- **MFL:** translation work
- **IT:** visual presentations of the planned rescue
- **Citizenship:** celebrating the success of the rescue

These are just ideas, but may be worth breaking down a little. As I touched on above, I sometimes come across the opinion that Drama is somehow at the other end of the learning spectrum to subjects like Maths or Science. Drama is somehow seen as trivial and, because it is something requiring *action* (like PE), it is easy, playful and only valuable in the sense that it builds confidence (apparently) and is 'good for you'. So to explore the story of the Chilean miners using Drama as a vehicle is all very nice in itself, but the perception is that the learning is shallow. I hope the list above counters the 'shallow' argument, but I also want to demonstrate that vigour and rigour can be there when hooking up Maths with the story.

A Maths teacher in the United States, Minerva Tavera, lined her kids up on the school's baseball pitch to create a true representation of what 700 metres actually looks like. The miners were trapped 700 metres below ground so she wanted her pupils to see this, to truly visualise how far this is. Being in the US, she also wanted to convert the distance into feet (1 m = 3.28 ft). It took around 600 students to create the image. The impact on the students, aged between 12 and 13, was tangible and many of them blogged about it. Minerva Tavera even convinced another 'serious' subject area, Science, to look at the effect of darkness on the health of the miners, whilst Health classes looked at heat, humidity and air supplies and how those would affect the men. Social Studies looked at the impact of the media on the future lives of the survivors.

Essentially, a curriculum emerged from a real event and could be hooked into the teaching and learning that was happening anyway.

Let's think beyond the trapped miners:

Where's the Maths and Numeracy* in:

- Planning a holiday
- Baking a cake
- Creating a superhero
- Enlarging a photograph
- Building a scale model
- Rescuing a threatened seal colony
- Moving the stones to build a pyramid
- Staging the Olympic Games
- Designing a roller coaster
- Cutting down a tree
- Planting a forest

(* Insert a subject area of your choice – try the same list with Science)

Going back to my own classroom experience described in this chapter with the children in Doncaster, there are some further details that need to be highlighted:

 Engagement strategies I used

1 **Altering the status quo:** *Can you get up and come to the front of the room please?* Huddle!

2 **Teacher fallibility:** *What miners?*

3 **Really ace questioning:** *I don't know much about this. Can you tell me more?*

4 **Tolerating hilarity:** Finding things they find funny, funny

5 **Being agreeable:** *Of course you can show your conversations!*

6 **Tolerating uncertainty:** *Of course (you can invent something that's never been invented before)*, aka going with the flow of the lesson

7 **Differentiating roles/creating a diversion:** *Josh! Jordan! You're in charge!*

8 **Connecting back to the start of the session making it all make sense:** *Huddle. It's dark. There's not much light but enough to see the letters we've written before we send them up*

9 **Inductive language:** The use of *we* (see number 8)

10 **Smiling and positive body language:** Even when Jordan and Josh were attempting to wind me up during the early stages of the session

Ten things we didn't learn at all

1 Where the heck Chile is

2 What the miners were mining for

3 Their names or dates of birth

4 How far underground they were

5 The date of the accident

6 The date of the rescue

7 How the miners were brought to the surface

8   How much of the Internet is given over to their story

9   How to do a PowerPoint capturing the above information

10 How to make a poster about the facts behind the Chilean miners' story

Ten things we did learn and that will be transferable to other areas of learning

1   We don't need a textbook

2   That Drama is not just making up plays and dressing up

3   What it is like to sustain people's spirits

4   To solve problems creatively

5   To present ideas enthusiastically

6   Being trapped down a mine isn't great

7   How to write for purpose from the point of view of a Chilean miner

8   Language of reassurance, inspiration and hope

9   That we can all contribute; that what we have to say is valued

10 That teachers don't know everything

Technology we used

We didn't really use any technology apart from big paper and fat pens. We could perhaps have used www.youtube.com to get some footage of the miners, but the whiteboard wasn't connected to the Internet. I didn't need it anyway. The children knew what we were talking about. Technically, they were the experts on it.

Protection into learning offers a way of luring young people into the learning that needs to be done. It also enables us to tap into the BRAVE curriculum mentioned above: we can allow our students to connect with subject matter that is **R**elevant, **A**cademic, **V**ocational and **E**valuatory. We can also use our really ace questioning skills to dig deeper. Put all this in the melting pot and you have the opportunity to lure learning and get committed engagement from the young people you are working with. I've illustrated a three-step route here but don't forget the other important elements when attempting to hook kids in. Here's a checklist:

- Routine entrance into classroom

- Good classroom management

- Clear introduction – objectives for the session could be shared here if you feel you want to, but don't ruin the journey

- A change from the norm – moving the desks perhaps or rearranging the seating plan. It's fair to say that if you do this every day it becomes the norm itself, but this way of inducting children into learning doesn't need to be like this all the time. It may be that you do this as a launch into a particular topic and that's it

- Step 1: A paired activity that engages, followed by a sharing of work

- Step 2: A paired or group activity that pushes the learners more; one that requires more thought, negotiation and, perhaps, compromise

- Step 3: An individual activity building on the previous two, where the pupil demonstrates their understanding of the topic

In terms of value, as the class moves through the steps, so the value increases: Step 1 is of low value but is important in that it is where the children find their feet and are able to experiment with what they already know about a theme. Step 3 is of high value as it is where the children, using Bloom's Taxonomy, create something new and become invested in the topic.

Here are three other examples of the three steps. Have a think about what areas of the curriculum are tapped into with these scenarios.

Older kids

1 School is setting up a student council. Conversation between students about what powers it will have

2 The local council has decided to close the school due to cutbacks and falling roll. Present the argument for keeping the school open to council officials

3 The date for the shutting of the school has been published. Plan a cross-media campaign/protest to keep the school open

Younger kids

1   You have found a time machine. Conversation between you and your friend about where you think you'd like to go in it

2   A fire destroys a house down the road. Prepare the instructions for the fire investigators to use your time machine to help prevent the fire from happening

3   When you have a time machine, what rules do we need to have in place for it to be used positively? Prepare these rules for publication

Even younger kids

1   We're off to the moon. Tell your partner why you need to go

2   The moon has no air to breathe. Design what you will wear that will help you breathe and explore safely

3   There are friendly aliens living on the moon. Create a banner that explains what you want the aliens to know about you and the human race

Can you visualise some learning you are planning with your class that can use this method:

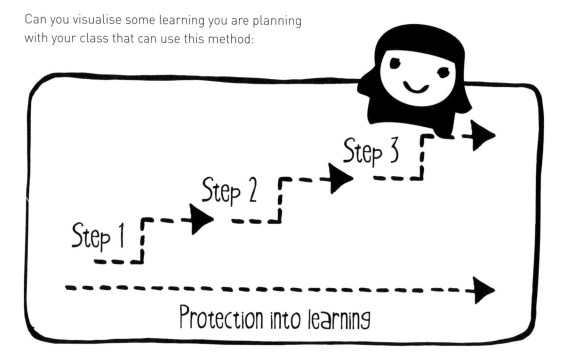

Much of what I've shared here relies on classroom management skills being well honed and good relationships existing in the classroom. If you've read the preceding chapters and acted on what I've offered there, you will be well on the road to getting excellent engagement in your classroom. Instead of just stepping up task work, a context is constructed, like a protective bubble surrounding you and your children in which the learning can happen. Here, physical hooks into learning (props, voices and pictures) act as tools of engagement and make the kids punch the air and cry 'Yes!' when you walk into the room – for all the right reasons.

- When all around you are losing theirs

Holding Your Nerve

Make decisions from the heart and use your head to make it work out.

Sir Girad

In Chapter 2 I talked about a BRAVE curriculum that is

- Buzzing

- Relevant

- Academic

- Vocational

- Evaluatory

It's all very well having acronyms to help us along, but all of these ideas, tools and strategies only work if the teacher is *up for it*. By being *up for it* I mean that in addition to confidence and permission from the powers-that-be, teachers need the *will* to innovate their classrooms and schools. Lesson planning is vital to ensure depth of learning and inclusivity of all children in the journey, it shouldn't however be a paper-prison from which there is no escape. Inspectors want to see you *facilitating* the learning whilst firing children's curiosity and passion for it. Risk-taking can be scary but without it nothing changes.

Top 10 Concerns for embracing learning accidents and employing inductive teaching methods for class teachers

1   The kids will go mental

2   I will go mental

3   The focus of the learning will blur

4   Learning objectives will not be met: the ones written on my board and on my lesson plan

5 The school inspectors will take me to the cleaners

6 My line manager will think I've lost it

7 The kids aren't used to working in this way so will be difficult to hook in

8 I'm going to run out of ideas

9 There's not enough time to do this sort of thing

10 The school leadership will think I'm a loose cannon and I'm really not!

Top 10 **Concerns for embracing learning accidents and employing inductive teaching methods for *school leaders***

1 Parents may not understand the change to a (perhaps) more creative agenda

2 Children may become unruly and lose the established focus on learning

3 Things that work may be dismissed in favour of approaches that don't

4 Ofsted may not like what they see

5 Children need to understand what it is they are learning so there needs to be a real coherence around the learning journey the teacher is taking them on

6 Writing opportunities, alongside other core subject areas, will be diminished

7 Children will see learning as fun so it will make it more difficult for other colleagues to teach them as expectations will be raised

8 It's too noisy

9 It's too tiring

10 There isn't time

I've heard all of these from school leaders in my time, particularly the last three. I've also met and worked with an overwhelming number of school leaders who have grasped the creative mettle and allowed their staff to run with it, champion it and enable their children to benefit from it. This may be the case in your school. Or maybe not. If it's not, then it may be up to you to be the Trojan Mouse – the teacher who doesn't hang about waiting for the next government educational directive, but gets on with making a difference in their own classrooms in the ways that I've described in this book. Of course, it's nicer to do this if you feel you've got the permission from your school leaders.

Just to break down some of the anxieties expressed earlier, it's good to see that the concerns expressed by class teachers and school leaders are similar.

Kids going bonkers
You can find advice in Chapter 7 for ways to protect children into learning, but can I also remind you of the need to have firm expectations and consistent routines in place. Kids go bonkers if you relinquish the control you have as the leader of learning in the classroom. You can keep this authority but still pass the ownership of the learning journey over to the children as I've described. At no point am I advocating the teacher walking into the classroom and greeting the children with:

What do you want to do today?

Because we are in control, we can create climates of learning that *appear* improvised and 'building the plane whilst flying it', but in fact, we are inducting the class by offering them responsibility and independence. The plan is in place but the directions and diversions are vaguer. *Kids go bonkers* is my way of describing children who have been stirred up by a teacher who has lost control. I've been there, and I don't want to go back there, thanks. But we are in charge: we hold the locus of control and never relinquish it. What we are happy to do is give opportunities to go with the flow of the learning. This is a skilled act, but one that is achievable for all teachers.

Holding on whilst letting go
The ability to suspend disbelief and grip the children in a context is such a fantastic (and democratic) way of opening up learning. For example, asking a child what a young man in a First World War trench may have in his kitbag can open up an oasis of learning opportunities. Where does the curriculum lie in this instance?

Here are the contents of his kitbag:

- A diary wrapped in a scarf
- A bible

- Photographs of family

- Photograph of friends in the trenches

- A lady's handkerchief

- A letter written by someone else

Can you see the talking points? The curriculum?

The letter written by someone else ...
The kitbag has been opened and the letter written by someone else is found and read. This, to me, opens up many opportunities:

- Who does the kitbag belong to?

- What do we learn about his life from the bag?

- Was he religious?

- What do we learn from the photographs?

- To whom did the handkerchief belong?

- What is written in the diary?

- Who has written the letter?

This idea emerged in a planning session in a school where the children needed a different sort of curriculum because they were the most vulnerable children in the town. So let's do some empathy work! Who has written the letter? Well, this is young Jim's kitbag and the letter within has been given to him by his pal to pass on to his family. Jim's friend has succumbed to the aftermath of the poison gas. So what's in his letter? If we get the children to create this letter (in the bag it's blank) ... what might 9-year-olds write? What might 12-year-olds write? What might 15-year-olds write?

We'll get to know the name of the writer when we see the name written at the end. Maybe, it's Billy. What do we know about Jim and Billy?

Can we create a *picture* of the moment Billy handed the letter to Jim, the owner of the kitbag? What does it look like?

A word about tableaux

This is a French word for creating a photograph of a moment in a story. If you look through the examples of learning contexts I've written up in this book, you should see loads of examples of where a tableau could be used. Don't panic if you're a Drama-hater (although if so, I'll be amazed if you got this far in the book). This is just a way of capturing a moment from which talking points can emerge – in the same way History textbooks share sources (original documents) with children – so we can create our own to analyse and pull apart.

The tableau is the most accessible Drama convention I know. It's a still image. A photograph. A situational moment where time is frozen. It's just so straightforward and there's no chance of any child being injured! It's open to you whatever subject you teach. Check out the following and see them as photographs:

- **Geography:** a family returning to their devastated home after the Japanese tsunami
- **English:** Atticus faces the mob outside the jail that holds the accused Tom Robinson (in Harper Lee's *To Kill a Mockingbird*)
- **Science:** the moment Edward Jenner injects the boy with smallpox to find out whether his vaccine theory is correct
- **Music:** the mosh pit at a Red Hot Chilli Peppers gig
- **Art:** an enactment of the Last Supper
- **Citizenship:** the protest against the closure of the library
- **History:** the trench on the Western Front during Christmas 1914

The only real rule is that when the children create the tableau, they must do so within the life of the people and circumstances they are depicting – you might have to find your own way of communicating this expectation. Basically, you can *protect* the children into this process quite easily by:

- Getting them to work in groups to create the tableau
- Giving them time to rehearse their depiction of the moment the learning is focusing on
- When viewing the tableau, we settle the audience and use the following convention to ensure a good effect

Audience (class) ready

The teacher counts down from 5 to 1; however, the class only hear the numbers 5 and 4 – numbers 3, 2 and 1 simply play in everybody's heads. Try it a few times – they'll get it! It's like the silence of 3-2-1 is a settler – it's a psychological contract that says that we are ready to watch and we are ready to perform.

We see the image and it is 'held' – that means, the children freeze and as the teacher we can invite the audience to comment on the tableau:

- What can you see?

- What is this man thinking?

- What is the future of these people?

- What might they be thinking here?

Basically, the tableau is a great way of creating an authentic focus of discussion no matter what age you teach. I've done tableaux with the youngest children we teach:

- Rescuing that scary cat from a tree: ages 5–7

- Discovering a dinosaur bone: ages 8–11

- The Pied Piper is rejected by the Mayor: ages 11–13

- Entering the gates of a haunted house: ages 14+

- The twins reuniting in Shakespeare's *Twelfth Night*: exam groups, post 16

Moving tableaux on

When discussing a tableau, give the 'performers' a moment to think about what the people they are representing might be thinking. Tell them you will tap them on their shoulder and, when you do, they should say what their character is thinking. For example, a tableau from the opening scene of *Hamlet* may depict the soldiers on the battlements witnessing the appearance of King Hamlet's ghost. The children are frozen in this depiction. You tap them each on the shoulder, allowing them all to speak before you move on. Now, I can't authentically predict what children might say. On the next page is an example of what I got when I did this very task recently.

Bernardo:	I'm so cold. And now this! Stuck out here in the freezing cold!
Marcellus:	I told you the ghost would come again!
Horatio:	What am I going to tell the Prince? He'll go mental.

The thing is, the children will find the words they need to speak much easier than if you were to ask them when they are sitting behind their desks. Tableaux let them project their own imaginations onto the characters they have physically created in their images. This is also a great way to deepen an understanding of empathy. And we all want our children to have that, don't we?

Another device you can deploy when using tableaux is to invite the participants to name the image they have created, much like a photographer names the photographs they take. This *title* can be used in creative ways.

How to use tableau titles

- **Before we see the image:** The children reveal their title and then the countdown from 5 happens with the 3-2-1 being silent, merely playing in everyone's heads. Giving the title offers a sense of anticipation for the rest of the class and is actually a really good settler in itself.

- **Within the image:** After the image is revealed, one of the participants says the title. This has the effect of making something that is initially unclear meaningful. This happens when an image is revealed and the class react with a kind of unanimous 'What the hell is this?' (you included). When the title is spoken, the class (and you) then see what the participants intended.

- **Just prior to the close of the image:** We look at the image and understand it. When we hear the title, our understanding of the image is challenged. Here's an example:
  - » Group of six participants
  - » One lies on the floor being hit, kicked and generally bullied by two others
  - » Another participant stands watching and smiling
  - » Another stands to the far left, facing away from the (frozen) action, sipping coffee from a cup, unaware of what is happening
  - » The final participant is on the far right, looking frightened, like *he is next*

Can you picture it? If you can't, read it again.

Here's what the title could have been, and what we in the audience would have put money on it being: 'Bullying'. Or perhaps: 'Bullying is Horrible'. Or, this being in a school in Barnsley: 'Bullying is Rate Bad'.

After looking at the image the participants had created for around twenty-five seconds, this is the title we were given: 'Revenge of the Bullied'. Read through the bullet points above again. Can you see it? This was a clever little group who had pulled us into their tableau and we had believed all our assumptions on seeing the image without the title. Once the name had been revealed, I asked the group to do it again and I did the shoulder tapping, finding out what was going on in the minds of these characters. The 'final participant is on the far right, looking frightened, like *he is next*' in the description above really went to town when I tapped his shoulder, revealing that he was the bully's enforcer but now the tables had well and truly turned! There was a genuine opportunity here to bring this character out of the tableau and do some hot seating (see Chapter 4), so that's what we did. This, in turn, led to other rich avenues of enquiry. Another happy learning accident.

Another good thing about the tableau is the way it can be so easily captured digitally and displayed. When I first started teaching Drama we did this in a very analogue way which involved me, a 35 mm camera and about thirty rolls of film (which were on offer at Boots) and would cater for all the 12-year-old children I taught. The project was called Photo Love Story and was based on those photo-stories that used to appear in girls' weeklies such as *Jackie* and which are still lampooned in the likes of *Viz*. This being the early 1990s, digital technology was lacking so it was quite simply a case of doing the following:

- Children into mixed-sex groups (as much as possible)
- Plan on paper a photo love story set in school that is true to the examples given by the teacher
- This is storyboarded into six or seven possible photographs with speech bubbles and thought clouds that could be added later
- Practically put together the image for the photographs (whilst introducing the term *tableau*)
- Teacher takes a photo of each tableau

- Teacher gets down to Boots (other picture developing companies were probably available back then)

- Teacher waits around for two hours as the assistant doing the developing wonders why this teacher has got over 600 pictures of schoolchildren

- Teacher explains the project to assistant

- Assistant tells the teacher it wasn't like this when she was at school

- Teacher agrees, pays for the pictures, forgets to get a receipt and spends the rest of the evening organising the pictures into class groups

- Groups receive pictures and after the removal of all those little 'Your pictures will be better if you take your time' stickers and the subtle colouring-in of all the zombie-like red-eyes, the images are secured to a big sheet of sugar paper with a title emblazoned across the top. The groups have a lot of fun with this sort of thing, with titles like: Corridor Misunderstanding, Ronald and Juliet, You Just Don't Get Me, Terminated, The Twiglet Zone, She's Bonkers! and Jealous Guy Guy'

  Admit it: I had you at Corridor Misunderstanding

- Then it's time for plain paper, scissors and glue sticks. The thought clouds and speech bubbles are added and Bob is indeed your uncle with the creation of a display, a demonstration of the class understanding of *dramatic irony* and a really neat way of using tableaux

Nowadays, of course, it's easier with all the hardware and software on offer to us as teachers (you could start at www.microsoft.com/photostory). Having said this, there is still something great about creating this sort of collaborative work and using the old technology.

If you're worried about your ideas drying up, chuck in some tableaux and see what can happen!

Now, where were we? Ah yes,

Holding your nerve

Take a look at this:

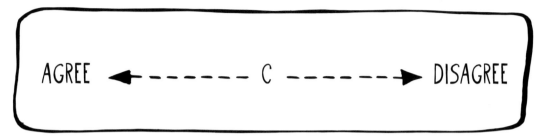

Now, imagine you're standing at the centre (C). I'm going to offer some statements to you. If you agree then you move along the spectrum towards *agree*. If you disagree, you move towards *disagree*. Here's one to get you going:

• I like Marmite

This is a good starter as it divides everyone! Now, for you reading this book, you can shift to wherever you feel you should be. If you've never tasted Marmite, you'll stay on the C.

Now try these statements which I've made up especially for you. After each one, move along the spectrum:

• I'm a good learner

• I'm confident in my practice

• I'm good at sharing

• I like my school

• My school likes me

Okay? Let's keep going then. Try these:

• I'm happy in this profession

• I'm treated as a professional

• I'm professional

• I need to learn more about my subject

• Teacher training prepared me well for this job

- I will always teach

- I will always learn

- When things go well, I share

- When things go wrong, I share

- My school supports me

- I support my school

- I'm looking forward to September

- I'm looking forward to August

- I'm often anxious

- I'm confident in my practice

I know you're doing this in your head, but it's also a really good thing to do with colleagues and children alike. Here are a few more I like to throw in when working with teachers:

- I absolutely believe in free speech for everyone

- Extreme political parties should be allowed to broadcast party political broadcasts on prime-time television

- I hate football

- I love sport

- I can visualise my retirement

- I will always do this job

- Recently, I have cried

- I have lied in the last five minutes

This is an extremely good way of finding out what the heck is going on with your staff. If you're a school leader for instance, you could ask the following:

- I feel listened to

- I trust the leadership of the school

You may think there's no way people would reveal their true feelings to you in response to those two statements if they were unhappy. And you're right! They wouldn't, unless you had properly established the protocol for doing this which is:

This is non-judgemental. Just go where you believe you belong at this time, on this day. You don't have to support your move with an explanation and you won't be asked to explain it by anyone else.

If this is made clear, the result is simply a barometer reading of the climate of your school. I'll come back to some leadership issues in a moment, but first, here are some statements I use with senior children who are at risk of failing some of their final school examinations. Notice I still start with the Marmite statement:

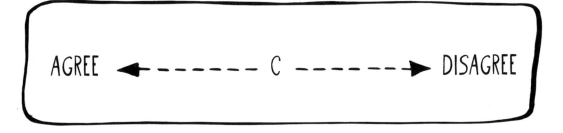

- I like Marmite

- I like school

- School likes me

- I know what I'm good at

- I've got good friends

- I'm just like my friends

- This time next year we'll still be mates

- Nothing changes

- I can change nothing

- I'm in charge of my own potential

- I'm looking forward to leaving school

- Being happy is more important than being rich

- Being successful is hard work

- I'm a grown-up

- I don't want to be a grown-up

- I need others to make my decisions

- I understand the qualifications I need to do what I want to do

- I'm worried about my exams

- I sometimes put my head in the sand and ignore what is obvious

- I know what I want to do with my life

- I know where to go for help

- I have heroes

- I don't have talent

- I know how to revise

- I hate revising

- I can work at home

- I'm always getting nagged at school

- I understand why I'm nagged

- I'm hard done to

- I'm lucky

- I have lied in the last two minutes

Think of a topic, a subject or a staff training event that you need to deliver. How could the agree/disagree process help you?

Is it *progress*?

One last thing on this: when you've got school inspectors in or are being observed (and judged), could you perhaps use this agree/disagree process as a starter and then deliver the lesson using the process once again at the end as a kind of plenary? I imagine that by using some carefully worded statements you would be able to get the children to demonstrate their progress since the beginning of the lesson. Just an idea. Here's another one when we're thinking about *showing progress*.

Progression chains

- Pupils write what they know about a topic on strips of paper

- Stick the ends of the strips together to make a loop

- Add to other loops

- A chain is created

- Stick this chain to your ceiling so it dangles

- As learning progresses, more links are added to the chain, showing progress

- At Christmas, birthdays and other celebrations, you can pin the dangling chain up on the ceiling and, hey presto! Instant decorations! What's not to like about that!

Also, don't let those individual pupil whiteboards gather dust in your cupboard. They were quite the thing before we were all consumed by interactive whiteboards. Dig them out and get the pupils using them. Get them to answer a question *wrong* at the start of the lesson, writing it on their own whiteboard. Then do your learning and teaching. Finally, get them to have a go at answering the key question again – this time *correctly*.

Now that's progress! Jazz hands everybody!

A quick word about inspection ...

Showing progress to inspectors is always a challenge for us in the classroom. When endeavouring to be BRAVE, it's essential we try our best to do so. Why? Because inspectors are in school to measure us, our children and our school and make judgements about everything we do. We are in it together, so there really isn't room for either loose cannons or grumpy gits who hate kids. Innovation in practice and curriculum has to happen with the support of those around us; there's no point in stressing out our line managers – what we need to do is dazzle them with the fruits of our labours.

It's clear that permission to innovate needs to come from the top and can make for really fertile ground from which to grow exciting teaching and learning. You'll have noticed that this is a theme of this book: be creative and seek the support of those around you and, even more importantly, above you. The three key elements around curriculum leadership (and beyond) could be seen as:

1 **Expectation:** In the senior role, this can be interpreted as an *approach* to the role which is professional, positive and open, rather than wandering around with your fingers crossed.

2 **Passion:** This is the viral infection that helps everyone in an organisation face in the same direction. It is not blind, but visionary.

3 **Energy:** This is the electricity that trumps the lack of time everyone in education feels. We may lack time, but do we really lack the energy?

These elements, or attributes, should be modelled by those who lead us. If we in the classroom don't see this, then it's even harder for us to be innovative, although we shouldn't stop trying. Innovation can be felt sometimes as top down, even though as innovators in the classroom it can often feel like bottoms up! If leaders get it right, it has a positive effect on the teaching staff and in turn this has an effect on the kids we teach.

When thinking of inspection, I'll also direct you to Jackie Beere's book *The Perfect Ofsted Lesson*. In it she writes:

[T]he role of the teacher when it comes to developing independence in the learner is that of knowledgeable, highly skilled mentor who is passionate about giving students the skills to find out for themselves.

When inspectors come a-knocking, show them what your children are capable of under your classroom leadership. Importantly, don't spend your year *anticipating* their arrival. Hanging about waiting for them, or waiting for the latest government initiative to take root, can really slow the progress of your class down.

When inspectors call into your room

1 Hang on to the principles you hold dear in terms of teaching and learning in your classroom

2 Don't be flash

3 Ensure previous great work is there to be seen on the walls, in journals and online

4 Resist the temptation to ask the visitor to play the part of the alien who has crash-landed on the school field

5 Stick to school policies (e.g. if you have to display WALT (We Are Learning To) and WILF (What I'm Looking For), do it) but ensure the teaching is yours. By this I'm referring to the received schemes of work we could easily regurgitate; *own the learning*

6 If the visitor arrives when things appear chaotic, proceed and, when appropriate, ask the children to talk through what they've been doing – this will translate into a mini-plenary before you move on

7 Don't feel you have to sum up the lesson on the visitor's arrival. You should probably provide them with a lesson outline though – that'll do the trick

8 When dealing with a challenging class who take their time in getting lured in, give them time to get orientated to your classroom – stick *orientation time* on your lesson plan just prior to your starter. This may manifest itself as those settling conversations you have with children when they arrive and when you are allowing them to catch up with each other. At the earliest possible moment though, get cracking

9 Show you are differentiating – by task, by outcome and by support

10 Don't swear or wink at the visitor

Obvious maybe, but here are some other things to consider

1 Governments change

2 Policies change

3 Curriculum fashions are cyclic – the Arts currently appear out of favour, but they'll be back

4 Systems of success-measurement develop

5 Teachers will always be held accountable

6 Children will always need teaching

7 The runaway train of technology development will keep rattling on

8 People will always revere the *old* methods and be highly suspicious of the *new*

9 Most people have been to school so are therefore experts on education

10 We constantly need to raise standards, because nobody wants to lower them

And finally ...

Okay, I'm wrapping things up but I'm finding it difficult! Get a pen. You're the one who knows how this story ends.

1 Be BRAVE

2 Have clear expectations

3 Fight passive imagination

4 Hold on whilst letting go

5 Objectives and outcomes can just be bookends to great experiences

6 Don't become one of The Ungrateful Dead. Get your pen. I'll leave the remaining four points for you to fill in.

7 --

8 --

9 --

10 --

There you go. If you've filled them in, then that's the psychological contract we have between us. Go and do what you've promised. Get out there and make a difference. Thanks for reading this to the end. You've done so because you're bothered, and the children will remember you fondly for it.

Some final thoughts from our sponsors:

I had a lot of trouble with engineers, because their whole background is learning from a functional point of view, and then learning how to perform that function.

Brian Eno

It's a miracle that curiosity survives formal education.

Albert Einstein

Useful Resources

www.createlearninspire.co.uk

www.dorothyheathcote.org

www.independentthinking.co.uk

www.janehewittphotography.co.uk

www.karenardley.com

www.kilda.org.uk

www.learningandteaching.info/learning/solo.htm

www.mantleoftheexpert.com

www.natd.eu

www.alistairsmithlearning.com

www.hywel.posterous.com

www.philbeadle.com

www.thunks.co.uk

As an added extra, I'm going to offer you my current top ten sites that are really supporting teaching and learning in my classroom today. They are also great for hooking and luring children into learning – I've suggested some examples on how to below. Check 'em out! I'm no technical genius – I've just picked these sites up along the way and I'm sharing them with you. There will be better ones around later today and most definitely I'll discover more interesting ones tomorrow, but until then, here you go.

Useful sites that can inspire you to hook kids into stuff

When reading this, remember none of it replaces you, the human teacher!

1   www.twitter.com

- The home of your personal learning network. This is an essential tool for any educator as it offers immediate peer-to-peer professional development. Get signed up immediately!

- It's a great place to get inspiration and practical ideas from colleagues around the world

- Need a picture of a moose with its antlers trapped in some overhead power cables? You'll find it here! Well, I did. Made my 13-year-old students shut up!

- Don't know your PISA from your RAISEonline? Ask your PLN!

- Get kids in your class into conversations with like-minded classes all over the world

2   www.glogster.com

- This is a great site for making fantastic posters for your classroom displays. It has a basic teacher account that will enable fifty of your students to upload work. With regard to expectations, this would be a great site to use in order to display *how* you want your classroom to run

3   www.posterous.com

- An excellent blogging site. It's essentially a high-speed email account where you can share everything from documents to videos. You can run it as a public group (where everyone in the world has access) or as a private group. The private group is great for class blogging and is a neat way of circulating ideas, thoughts, task work, rewards and celebration. It is also useful to gather thinking and research evidence when working as a team of professional colleagues

4   www.oneword.com

- Reluctant writers? Lazy literati? The site does what it says. It chucks a word out at you and gives you sixty seconds to write as creatively as you can about it, around it, through it, over it and so on

- The words it picks out as your muse can be hilarious. For example, you have one minute to write about: bacon, intense, lampshade, mirror ... Have a go, it's cool!

- All work can be uploaded so there's a great opportunity to share and celebrate

- This is a fab site to let children have some fun with writing

5   www.blogger.com

- A great blogging site which is easy to use

- There are many teachers using sites such as Blogger and Posterous to set up class blogs on which to share learning. These groups use Twitter to publicise their work

- I've just found a site called www.classblogs.us which also looks good!

6   www.youtube.com

- The granddaddy of video uploading. Blocked by some schools and local authorities like an Internet postcode lottery

- My GCSE Media Studies class used to get around local authority blocks by logging into YouTube via Germany (www.youtube.de). You didn't hear that from me ...

- Also check out channels available on YouTube. Recommended are: ITL Worldwide and YouTube Teachers. All you need to do is sign up to the site

7   www.voki.com

- This site allows your pupils to create avatars (characters) for themselves that are animated online

- The kids can upload their own voice recordings for the avatar to perform online. This supports those reluctant to speak up or present in class. It's also good fun and an interesting addition to presentations, as well as an innovative way to present Pupil Voice

- Voki has been used really successfully in MFL lessons as a way of engaging the disaffected (and trapping them into learning!)

8 www.toondoo.com

- Here you can create cartoons. Basically it's a load of clip art to which you can add speech and thought

- You can also create characters and customise what's on offer by adding your own arty touches to the characters supplied

- Useful for revision, capturing ideas and illustrating arguments

- I saw it used really well recently with a class of children with special educational needs

9 www.storybird.com

- Not dissimilar to ToonDoo in that illustrations are offered to support your own text

- A great way of supporting and presenting children's writing

- Finished books can be added to online libraries and shared

- Hard copies of books can also be ordered – they're pricey but beautiful

- In terms of hooking children, it's another site that can engage reluctant writers by essentially saying 'Here are the pictures, now tell us the story'

10 www.photofunia.com

- A photo site that offers effects that you can apply to your own saved images. Great for adding kids' mugshots into backgrounds (e.g. a painting in an art gallery or a billboard). Go and have a look and you'll see what I mean. It's slightly addictive. Also a right laugh!

Some older junior pupils I was working with recently also recommended www.educationcity. com but it's a subscription site which means it will cost the school. They liked it a lot. Many of these sites require you to sign up and share your creations. As Mark Zuckerberg, Facebook's young inventor says: 'We're building toward a web where the default is social.' So, essentially, it's all about sharing. Your pupils will be happy uploading work; you may need to 'let go' a little and not insist on all work being present and evidenced in an exercise book or folder.

Get on Twitter and find us then we can all share the latest cutting-edge thinking, strategies and tools we need to be the best educators we can be:

@hywel_roberts

@thatiangilbert

Bibliography

Anderson, L. (2005) *A Taxonomy for Learning, Teaching and Assessing: A Revision of Bloom's Taxonomy of Educational Objectives*. London: Pearson.

Beere, J. (2010) *The Perfect Ofsted Lesson*. Carmarthen: Crown House Publishing.

Biggs, J. B. and Collis, K. F. (1982) *Evaluating the Quality of Learning*. Maryland Heights, MO: Academic Press, Inc.

Black, P. and Wiliam, D. (2006) *Inside the Black Box*. Slough: NFER Nelson.

Blanchard, K., Zigarmi, P. and Zigarmi, D. (1999) *The One Minute Manager: Leadership and the One Minute Manager.* London: Harper.

Bloom, B. S. (1956) *Taxonomy of Educational Objectives, Handbook I: The Cognitive Domain*. New York: David McKay Co., Inc.

Fullan, M. (2001) *Leading in a Culture of Change*. San Francisco, CA: Jossey-Bass.

Gilbert, I. (2007) *The Little Book of Thunks*. Carmarthen: Crown House Publishing.

Goleman, D. (1996) *Emotional Intelligence: Why It Can Matter More than IQ*. London: Bloomsbury.

Heathcote, D. and Bolton, G. M. (1995) *Drama for Learning: Dorothy Heathcote's Mantle of the Expert Approach to Education* (Dimensions of Drama Series). Portsmouth, NH: Heinemann.

Rogers, C. (1951). *Client-Centered Therapy: Its Current Practice, Implications and Theory*. London: Constable.

Smith, J. (2010) *The Lazy Teacher's Handbook*. Carmarthen: Crown House Publishing.

Tayabali, R. *Managing Different Types of Agile Team*. http://consultingblogs.emc.com/rizwantayabali. (accessed 27 March 2012).

Wragg, E. and Brown, G. (1993) *Questioning* (Leverhulme Primary Project: Classroom Skills). London: Routledge.

Index